Mastering Leadership Alignment

Mastering Leadership Alignment

Linking Value Creation to Cash Flow

J.W. Ballard
Andrew Bargerstock, CPA

 BUSINESS EXPERT PRESS

Mastering Leadership Alignment: Linking Value Creation to Cash Flow
Copyright © Business Expert Press, LLC, 2017.

First published in 2017 by
Business Expert Press, LLC
222 East 46th Street, New York, NY 10017
www.businessexpertpress.com

ISBN-13: 978-1-63157-503-7 (paperback)
ISBN-13: 978-1-63157-504-4 (e-book)

Business Expert Press Supply and Operations Management Collection

Collection ISSN: 2156-8189 (print)
Collection ISSN: 2156-8200 (electronic)

Cover and interior design by S4Carlisle Publishing Services
Private Ltd., Chennai, India

First edition: 2017

10 9 8 7 6 5 4 3 2 1

Printed in the United States of America.

Dedication

*With deep gratitude to Andy Bargerstock who made this book possible, the book is dedicated to five people who have made huge impacts on my life and work. The first two are Louis "Lou" Mobley (mob-lee)—author of **Beyond IBM (1988)** and discoverer of the Mobley Matrix and ROA Chart—and Charles "Chuck" Kremer—author of **Friendly Finance, Finally (1997)**, lead author of **Managing by the Numbers (2000)**, and inventor of the Financial Scoreboard. Without their friendship and support as colleagues, we would not have been able to do what we are doing today, and have been doing since 1986. Their work has provided a foundation to contribute breakthrough leadership through business and finance alignment practices.*

*The third and fourth are my parents: My father, the late John W. "Jack" Ballard, modeled for me what it means to be a steward in all areas of life. Jack was a civic leader, human potential pioneer, and a Fortune 25 human resources executive. As a father and partner in life he had more impact on me than perhaps he knew. My mother, Phoebe Ballard Ford, bestowed unconditional love, support, persistent and unflagging encouragement, and awesome generosity. These continue to be foundational constants helping me share my gifts to servant leaders. The writing of their book, originally titled **Beating the Age Game (1994),** and now called **Turning Points (2002, 2006),** and their seminars supporting people to be purpose-driven while transitioning from a career into "The New Impermanence" modeled for me a commitment to be proactive in offering the gifts of their experience and wisdom to the world.*

*Lastly, to my astonishing great grandfather, David McConaughy, whose books **Pioneering with Christ (1941), Mother Earth: Studies in Stewardship (1929),** and **Money: The Acid Test (1919)** have been such beacons for me from this great gentlemen I never knew in person. David spent a dozen years in Madras, building the YMCA in India, now the city of Chennai, where this book has been produced. As Jack used to sign his correspondences on occasion*
— All power to those who care.

—J.W. (Jahn) Ballard

Abstract

Mastering Leadership Alignment (MLA) shows how to align senior teams to move their enterprise in unanimity toward greater levels of adept business execution. This book conveys powerful methods, with real-world case stories for guiding Senior Leadership to dramatically improve enterprise results through continuously generating whole-hearted unanimity on core facts. This method is derived from decades of direct experience through more than 50 consulting engagements in building collaborative cultures of engaged leaders and staff in commercial and community enterprises.

The unobstructed path to MLA requires solving classic issues that thwart alignment. Two of the seven discoveries that are revealed and resolved are:

More than 50 percent of enterprise value-creating assets reside in undocumented tacit employee knowledge about business processes.

CEO and CFO roles suffer from a built-in structure that generates dissonance and erodes alignment.

Any senior leader or facilitator can use this learning guide to build whole-hearted senior team unanimity on core facts of enterprise.

MLA is for enterprising professionals: senior leaders, trusted advisors to senior leaders and their direct reports, facilitators of change, and students of business-building competencies.

Contents

Templates, Chapter Exhibits Appendices with Activity Statement
Samples available at
www.MOSupgrade.com/MLA/Library

Preface
The Missing Methodology

by Andrew Bargerstock

It is widely accepted that a new management paradigm is needed to meet the challenges of rapidly changing market conditions and technological advances. Executives, professional associations, and academics promote new thinking about how to successfully transform business strategy into effective operations. Many books offer principles-based guidance on this subject. But few, if any, provide a systematic, step-by-step approach to closing the gap between planning and implementation. This void in management education has existed for a long time.

While pursuing my MBA in the early 1970s, I first recognized **a critical weakness in business education**. Colleagues at other business schools reported the same observation. We had all received good training in strategic planning, operations management, marketing, finance, business law, human resource management, and other business disciplines. But, nowhere did we learn how to align a business' value streams congruently with the unique operational success drivers of the enterprise. This elusive element is what I called the **Missing Methodology**.

After my MBA studies, I worked as an auditor with a large CPA firm in Pittsburgh, PA, where I was fortunate to observe a variety of business practices, some highly successful and others that yielded more modest results. Each enterprise relied heavily on financial statements to provide some level of feedback on the implementation of their business tactics. Top decision makers dug deeply into classic financial ratios and percentages such as return on sales, return on asset, inventory turnover, accounts receivable turnover, and times interest earned for guidance. Some insights were gained. But, the powerful linkages between employee behaviors and the desired results were often obscured. Sometimes this lack of linkages is overcome by labor-managed firms, in which all the employees are involved in the decision-making methodology, not just the "top decision-makers." Few organizations have developed valid key performance indicators (KPIs) that are monitored continuously to realign business priorities. Consequently, these businesses are not achieving the level of success to which they aspired.

Executive Perspective

Today, more than ever, executives are recognizing the gap between good strategic planning and the ability to implement with excellence. Creating a good business strategy is not sufficient for business success. Adept execution is required, if the energy and inspiration of great leadership are to be converted to its highest value-creating purposes. Recognizing the need, successful entrepreneur Naveen Jain (founder of InfoSpace and Moon Express) stated, "Success doesn't necessarily come from breakthrough innovation but from flawless execution. A great strategy alone won't win a game or a battle; the win comes from basic blocking and tackling" (Jain, 2016).

Professional Association Perspective

Professional associations in accounting and finance also acknowledge the need for change. In a 2014 white paper entitled, "Financial Insight: Challenges and Opportunities," and co-sponsored by both the Institute of Management Accountants (IMA) and the UK-based Association of Certified Chartered Accountants (ACCA), the authors call for heightened involvement of the finance function in bridging the gap between strategy and operations.

Sunil Golecha, CFO Thomson Reuters Asean and North Asia, put it this way, "Today's enterprise has to be much more entrepreneurial to drive growth in a competitive and volatile environment." Finding the appropriate business model "is not necessarily intuitive for the finance function. . . . We definitely need to be able to challenge the business but we need to do this in a way that does not prevent really innovative decision-making." (IMA, 2014)

On the basis of a series of world-wide open forums with financial executives, surveys, and interviews, the study concluded that the most important agenda point for CFO leadership is to understand the KPIs and activities that have most impact on business value, and focus business partnering activities in these areas. They call for finance executives to think more entrepreneurially (IMA, 2014).

Academics and Consultants Perspective

Academics also study the gap between strategy and implementation. In the 2005 Harvard Business Review article, "Turning Great Strategy into Great Performance," Makins and Steele indicate that **enterprises typically realize only about 60 percent of their strategy value due to "defects and breakdowns in planning and execution."** Additionally, these experts report that only about 15 percent of businesses take the time to compare business results to projections from their operational plan. As well respected as American business practices may be, there is significant room for improvement.

Makins and Steele identified **seven rules for successful execution of business strategy**:

- Keep strategy clear and simple.
- Challenge assumptions, not forecasts.
- Agree on a common language for assessing performance.
- Discuss resource deployments early.
- Identify and realign priorities.
- Continuously monitor performance and modify strategy as warranted.
- Reward execution abilities.

Following the seven rules is easier said than done! During my time as an executive with a Fortune 500 subsidiary, I observed well-intentioned senior managers beginning the year with reasonably well-defined business plans that had been developed in a collaborative manner with their teams. The first three rules were handled well. But, as the weeks moved ahead, there was inconsistent attention on the remaining four rules. Most managers got consumed in fighting fires, that is, their attention was drawn to issues of the day. The big picture slipped into the background, lost to the urgencies of the immediate term. By the last few months of the fiscal year, these same well-intended managers suddenly realized what they had been neglecting.

In 2005, I began to immerse myself in concepts of Lean Management and Lean Accounting. Through Lean methods, I saw the potential for developing a whole system, value-chain-oriented tool for linking strategy and tactics.

Toyota Motor Company has contributed significantly to the development of thought about Lean Management and especially the concept of kaizen (continuous process improvement). They have shared their experiences and expertise about how to identify business problems and solve them on the level of the shop floor. But they have been less than candid about middle and upper management practices related to Lean. Unnamed insiders report that Toyota does indeed possess a systematic method for connecting business plans to operations. But exactly how it works continues to be closely held.

Without doubt, this book provides the keys to the Missing Methodology through Ballard's Five Alignment and Reporting Disciplines (BARD), which act as a management operating system upgrade. This new engagement paradigm wakes up any organization to the previously untapped genius of its own workforce while systematically identifying priorities for cultivating enterprise excellence.

In their quiet moments, many executives know their organization could be achieving higher levels of performance. And they yearn for a systematic method to close the business performance gap. If these thoughts invade your quiet moments, read closely for a possible solution.

References

Jain, N. (2016). *10 Secrets of Becoming a Successful Entrepreneur.* Retrieved from http://www.inc.com/naveen-jain/10-secrets-of-becoming-a-successful -entrepreneur.html. Inc. Magazine.

IMA. (2014). Retrieved from http://www.imanet.org/about-ima/news-media -relations/ima-press-releases//14-09-09/Business-Centric_Approach _Increasingly_Important_for_CFO_Organizations_Says_ACCA_IMA _Report-2610432828

Foreword

By Tom Hood, CPA, CEO at Maryland Association of CPAs (MACPA)

"The greatest danger in turbulent times is not the turbulence. It is to act with yesterday's logic."

Peter Drucker

As CEO at MACPA, I always like to make sure I have got *good* information for our members, so as I scan and read I look for themes and patterns that can inform, support, and challenge what I am seeing emerge from my perspective. These days a lot of that research, and many of these themes and patterns show up in my social stream from Facebook, LinkedIn, Twitter, and in blogs I follow whose authors share what they see and think is important. That has happened a number of times as I have been thinking about the core subjects of this book. At MACPA, we have been implementing Lou Mobley, Chuck Kremer, and Jahn Ballard's methods since 2001, at both the leadership level and the whole staff level at our state association with 9,000 CPA members.

In an article about maps by bestselling author, Seth Godin (2012),[1] I see a highly relevant perspective on the challenges we all face in doing business. One of these noteworthy patterns is that for him, maps are becoming useless, as "the map keeps getting redrawn because it's cheaper than ever to go off-road, to develop and innovate and remake what we thought was going to be next." Moreover, "technology keeps changing the routes we take to get our projects from here to there. It doesn't pay off as much to memorize the route, because it's going to change soon."

In the "good the old days," just a few years ago, all we had were maps— no GPS. We used to drive to AAA or the convenience store for a map of that city or county, so we could figure out how to get where we were headed. For Seth, "the map isn't important. What we need now is a compass." I would go a step further. What we need now is a gyroscope! A gyroscope shows us where we are, even when we are upside down in the churn of a wave. So what is our gyroscope as businesspeople, and how do we use it?

"The new role of finance is to be the whole system connector that links finance to strategy and external stakeholders, while also providing line-of-sight from results in the past and intentions for the future, to all operating activities."

As a leader applying this material in enterprise for decades, this book shows us what business leaders can do to have their people and organizations guided by a gyroscope, that is, by a superior method of guidance. Combining operations, strategy, and finance provides a critical gyroscope needed to stay agile in today's fast-moving business environment. Ballard's methods provided us at MACPA the opportunity to develop an enterprise gyroscope for insightful guidance into our future. Here is what I told my whole staff at the beginning of a Management Operation System upgrade session we conducted in 2011 with Jahn Ballard's approach, 10 years after we began using Chuck Kremer and Lou Mobley's tools and methods with Jahn in 2001.

> *Over the last decade, we have been learning how to be great lookouts for our members. This continues to be an evolving process where each of you as staff people will always look out from your vantage point, and bring information back to leadership and each other, so we can use all the knowledge to make better decisions.*
>
> *Just like a big container ship, if leaders and staff think of all the 'containers' as value units going to a customer (external or internal), successful delivery requirements for all our 'value containers' can be understood. One can think of the red containers as one line of business—in our case it is Continuing Professional Education (CPE), where Jahn Ballard has delivered Accounting and Auditing classes on Three Bottom Line Performance to CFOs, Controllers and small-practice CPAs. One can think of the blue containers as another— in our case, Conferences. The green containers, another—for us our Customized Learning Services. Our Membership Services might be the white containers.*

What we did using Ballard's Alignment and Reporting Disciplines (BARD) was look at those value containers and ask ourselves—What is the sequence of value-creating activities we use to generate satisfied and loyal customers; and all our financial results? This primary question begs further questions—What's relevant to our members, and how is that changing? What will our members want in the future? How could we rearrange how many, and which value containers we have? How can we deliver that value to our members in the best possible way? You are our scouts who can use your knowledge to help navigate turbulent seas and adjust the business model as we go.

When I talk about our business model, it's really just about the things that we do to create value. Our job ideally is to be proactive about that, right? That's why, after working with leadership, we have engaged everyone in our whole system in seeing how the value containers they are responsible for connect to cash flow and profit margin results. We have needed to be thinking clearly about our future, not just our past.

Because there are always competitors out there, in our case for our members, and for the products and services that we provide to members, our learning speed needs to be greater than our competition.

(from Tom Hood address to MACPA employees in 2011)

And ideally, our learning speed ideally should also be equal to or greater than the rate of change itself. I want all my staff to have this attitude, whether they are near the front of the ship, in the bow, in the hold, on the sides, or in the stern.

Our Key Performance Indicator methods and our Three-Bottom-Line Analysis tools coupled with our vision, values, core competencies, and our overarching strategy actually provide us with a gyroscope. That means, with all the staff's help, we are navigators of market change. Our "gyroscope," with our new logo and our new identity that emerged so strongly out of a KPI Integration Launch with Jahn and our whole team, gives us definition and insight. Developing and validating our Chart of Activities, working with all the disconnects, and considering new KPIs with the whole staff (after working on that with our leadership) gave us our boundaries, and clarified what directions we are headed. No matter what the turbulence, this will point us in the right direction. It is not an external map, because it is not that clear exactly what the market territory looks like. I see our work together here at MACPA as the major "channel markers" that we stay within better and better. Now that we have our gyroscope, we are able to learn how to surf the waves more confidently and avoid the washing machine churn. We are continuously better able to ride these waves of change.

Our journey at the Maryland Association of CPAs (MACPA) over the past 15 years has been a journey of discovery, change, and adaptation. Beginning in 2001 with Three-Bottom-Line Performance, it has been full of continuous learning. Ballard's Alignment and Reporting Disciplines have been expanded to include our entire team, because for us the environment is simply too fast-moving and too turbulent to not enlist the wisdom of everyone. This book shares parts of our story with key tools and methods so that you can engage your senior team initially, to help them learn how to navigate change. When the senior team is in rock-solid agreement, you will figure out as the senior team how to engage the key stakeholders to unanimously focus together on creating value. I wish you a successful voyage.

Tom Hood, CPA, Maryland Association of CPAs' CEO

Reference

1. Godin, S. (2012). *The Map Has Been Replaced by the Compass.* Retrieved from http://sethgodin.typepad.com/seths_blog/2012/02/the-map-has-been -replaced-by-the-compass.html.

Introduction

A Management Operating System Upgrade

by Jahn Ballard

This book is for CEOs and CFOs, change management facilitators, entrepreneurs, and profit or not-for-profit enterprise managers and their allies, who seek a logical, clear path for guiding enterprises to achieve consistently improving performance. The models, methods, and tools offered in this book demonstrate how to implement a whole-systems methodology that directly connects strategy, finance, and operations, in alignment with enterprise value-creating activities.

Through 15 to 20 years of development in real-world situations, we developed a step-by-step methodology for closing the gap between operational planning and performance excellence, applicable to any kind of enterprise. The five Alignment and Reporting Disciplines are the methods. From decades of direct experience of what works, we share what we have learned about waking enterprises up to the value-creating resources that currently reside in their own people's tacit job knowledge and value creation wisdom. A Management Operating System (MOS) exists in every enterprise. It is the way the enterprise runs itself, in a systematic manner with sound policies and good internal controls—some of which are formal and some are informal. Unfortunately for many enterprises, much of the MOS is invisible. This book offers a path to making the MOS visible and useful to any engaged staff. The upgrade begins with the senior team coming to unanimity, that is, to an explicit and whole-hearted agreement on the current facts of value-creating activities and where they need to be improved.

Maybe you have found yourself in situations like these, where the senior team struggles because full alignment on a clearly prioritized path for guiding activities eludes them:

- The CEO and senior team are working their tails off, and the company is growing. The accountant shows the company is profitable. "Great bottom line last quarter." But there always seems to be a scramble to pay bills on time because there is not always enough cash in the bank. Why?

- Business was great last year, and the CEO wants to expand into a new facility. But the banker takes one look at the financials and shakes her head. "The enterprise hasn't got the cash flow to support the loan request." The CEO is puzzled—has not the enterprise performed well? What gives?

- A new competitor opened up down the street and the enterprise feels the pinch. Some cuts must be made—but where? Which product lines are least profitable? If people are let go, how much will be saved, given the lost value delivery capacity?

- A myriad of issues are fighting for attention from CEO and staff. How do we decide priorities for improvements within the time and budget available? How does one engage everyone else to do the same? There is too much complexity to do it all at once.

- Demand is scaling rapidly for the enterprise value proposition. Rapid and seem-less integration of new leadership and line teams has become a critical, time-sensitive priority.

- The CEO has led a successful team for decades, and has to think about handing off the ship to another captain. The CEO worries that a successful transition may not be in the cards.

- No matter what the scale of enterprise, the market is a lot less forgiving than it used to be. Margins are being pinched from multiple sides and sales growth is soft or leveling. There are several possible scenarios to consider in response, but one seems the most promising. How to quickly and accurately project cash flows for the next several quarters—without bothering your accounting office?

Integrated operational and financial information can help solve these problems and take advantage of more opportunities. In fact, an integrated picture can inform usefully on many of the tough decisions that enterprise owners and managers must make every day. One would not fly a plane without all the dials and gauges showing the heading and that everything's working the way it is supposed to. Similarly, one would prefer not to run an enterprise without the reports and information that show where things are on track, where they are not on track, and whether or not the enterprise is really creating enough operating cash.

Consider these questions:

Is there a complete picture of how all the operating activities in the enterprise fit together?

Is it clear which operating activities convert to which specific financial impacts?

Are all the constraints to value creation in the enterprise known? And of these critical value constraints, which most need repair, overhaul or transformation?

Are there operating cash to sales reports on the enterprise every month?

Do the financial reports show you clearly whether or not, and how cash has been added to, or subtracted from, cash reserves or internal investment funds?

Do the financial reports link directly to nonfinancial measures of what people actually do to create those results?

Does the senior team regularly and effectively meet to use the information in those reports to help make informed decisions about defining and driving the future financial and value-creating results for the enterprise?

If the answer to any one of these questions is "no," do not be alarmed. There are estimates that as many as 50 percent of small- and medium-sized company owners and managers do not get complete, or timely information about their enterprise's financial performance. Some say as many as 90 percent do not fully understand or use the information provided. Larger organizations also struggle with these issues in a myriad of often-invisible or isolated ways.

In any case, if you answered "no" to any of our questions, we intend this book for you. We show how to gradually transform an enterprise into a more dynamic, engaged, customer-focused, and value-driven team. You will learn how to move leaders and staff into documentation and dialogue skills to determine key drivers of enterprise success, to develop and select appropriate metrics to monitor performance, and to participate in an ongoing healthy adventure to streamline processes and improve results.

Okay, so what is a key indicator of successfully implemented Ballard Alignment and Reporting Disciplines? Significant **improvement in cash flow from operating activities** is the signature indicator of successful implementation of the MOS Upgrade. Employee job satisfaction and better productivity are ancillary benefits that track with the financial improvements.

Let us clarify the purposes of this book.

First, this book is about developing meaningful measures of value-creating activities that can be linked directly to the reporting of financial results. People who run enterprises need to make sure that their accounting office (and their accounting software) gives their internal customers the information that is most relevant for decision making. In the real case studies presented in this book, you will see the wide range of financial and customer benefits.

Second, this book presents a unique approach to understanding both the operations and the finances of your enterprise in its entirety, as a foundation for building ever more whole-hearted unanimity. To institutionalize a culture of effective collaboration, we show how to engage the CEO and CFO in aligning, and then other senior leaders and eventually other colleagues.

Third, we know that every enterprise operating over the years has an existing and well-functioning MOS (how the enterprise does business that works). Experimenting effectively with the Alignment and Reporting Disciplines will inexorably upgrade that MOS, by bringing enterprise value creation know-how out from being invisible tribal knowledge and into being a prized asset and competitive advantage.

What You Will Learn

- **How to build an enterprise's value-creating activities sequence** through a Chart of Activities and Value Cycle Map that can be linked to the Chart of Accounts. These can continue to evolve, and help guide enterprise improvement year after year. As long as the right questions continue to be asked, and in the most effective sequence, greater unanimity can emerge.
- **How three specific bottom-line measures, one from each of the three financial statements, reveal an integrated perspective of enterprise financial performance.** A complete evaluation of enterprise financial performance requires perspective from all three bottom-lines. Operating cash in relation to sales is the primary reference point (the key financial driver) connecting the bottom lines.
- **How activity statements can inform about financial reality.** For a more complete picture of enterprise performance, develop one-page activity statements summarizing value creation measures. Consider which value-creating activities carried out by staff every day affect which transactions on the financial Chart of Accounts. It can be even more helpful when those who receive paychecks also understand which of their own and their colleague's daily activities affect which transactions, especially those affecting Cash Flow from Operating Activities accounts.
- **How to link activity statements and financial statements together, through a simple set of methods, and a mapping tool that links operating activities to the bottom lines.** The financial modeling that we offer was developed by the late Lou Mobley, a values innovator and financial software inventor who was also a pioneering executive leadership

school director at IBM. Mobley partnered with *Managing by the Numbers* author, Chuck Kremer, CPA, to create curriculum and tools that offer Cash Competency to finance professionals and business people. These Value-Creating Activity and transaction summary modeling tools are part of Ballard's Alignment and Reporting Disciplines.

- **How to enhance your skills and discipline for drawing out creative insights and plans from enterprise leaders, and then staff.** Building whole-hearted unanimity increases internal capacity to realize enterprise goals. When one asks skillfully for colleagues and key staff to share their deep understanding of business operations and insights for improvements, one unlocks vast creative potential while also enhancing job satisfaction.

In short, this is a book for facilitators, senior leaders, company owners, managers and staff, and serious students of business who want to know how to systematically guide an organization to achieve operational excellence by coherent understanding of enterprise value-creating activities.

Note: *Mastering Leadership Alignment*'s website provides additional no-fee templates and other resources for leadership alignment in enterprises. See www.MOSupgrade.com/MLA/Library to illustrate how enterprises have benefited from our approach.

We are using BARD as the abbreviation for Ballard's Alignment and Reporting Disciplines throughout.

So, roll up your sleeves. Let us dive in . . . !

Mastering Leadership Alignment

Linking Value Creation to Cash Flow

by Ballard and Bargerstock

How to understand and get the most out of this book

We have written this book primarily for four groups of business professionals: (1) senior leaders motivated to guide their core team toward unanimity and beyond, (2) trusted advisors to senior leaders and their direct reports, (3) facilitators who work with senior leaders on change management initiatives, and (4) any student of business who is building competencies for the day they will participate in senior leadership activities.

The seven assumptions that shape how we go about aligning senior teams to move their enterprise toward greater levels of adept business execution open this outline. We then summarize each chapter. Finally, we include key sources informing the evolution of each of those Seven Assumptions.

This book conveys a powerful story and method for guiding Senior Leadership to dramatically improving organizational results. We refer to this method as Ballard's Alignment and Reporting Disciplines (BARD). Here are the assumptions at the basis of this method.

Seven Assumptions Shaping BARD

Assumption 1. Existing unanimity about value creation is hidden in financials.

In every enterprise senior leaders desire a coherent unanimity of purpose and priorities that is often not realized. Undocumented, invisible, this unexpressed agreement remains consistently stranded. Yet, when sufficiently awakened, the coherent voice of senior leaders crystallizes into a significant enterprise asset. The financial statements' potential as a centerpiece for strengthening unanimity is often underutilized. The statements contain a core set of facts that can be discovered collaboratively, especially when linked and documented with a shared glossary (a common language) about total value creation.

Assumption 2. CEO and CFO roles have a built-in structure that generates dissonance.

Built-in structural dissonance can consistently thwart the CEO and CFO roles because of differences in business language, external influences and functional mindsets. These differences create dissonance, detracting from the potential of a shared and fully aligned business framework. We address this condition by developing basic measurement maturity skills for all enterprise leaders, while simultaneously applying the skills directly to serving current mandates. The CEO and CFO can find their points of whole-hearted unanimity on their core facts in a matter of hours and then in minutes.

Assumption 3. Alignment begins with Senior Leaders and cascades downwards.

The leadership team can discover and document their own agreement on value creation, key drivers, and a core set of unarguable facts. They can then continue to build ever-widening circles of aligned staff, who together can share and document increasingly complete and whole-hearted unanimity.

Assumption 4. Over 50 percent of enterprise value-creating assets reside in staff job knowledge.

Implicit, tribal, and invisible wisdom can be harvested, documented, reported, and then integrated to guide staff excellence in value-creating activities. *Deep Smarts* (2005) from Harvard Business School Press asserts that at least 50 percent of the value-creating assets of any enterprise reside in staff's undocumented, inherent work experience and tacit job knowledge.

Assumption 5. Whole-hearted unanimity springs from discovering core objective facts together.

When undocumented agreement gets recorded, whole-hearted unanimity can spring from the core objective facts discovered. Unanimity produces both a valuable foundation of leverage and a strong point of departure toward enterprise-wide alignment and excellence.

Assumption 6. Generally, there are one primary constraint and two to four secondary constraints in a complex work system.

In most organizations, effectiveness is thwarted by one primary constraint and two to four secondary constraints at any given time. A necessary prerequisite to identifying these few constraints (out of the total existing set of constraints) is first learning about where every one of the value-creating activities are breaking down. Once a total set of disconnects is assembled, collaborative analysis can begin.

Assumption 7. Any senior leader with requisite skills can build senior team unanimity.

Any senior leaders with requisite professional skills and/or sufficient training as a facilitator could use this book as a catalyst to build whole-hearted senior team unanimity. However, in many cases, one may be well advised to enlist the shadow support of an experienced facilitator, coach, or process consultant to help with customizing BARD to fit with the enterprise culture as congruently as possible.

The unfolding of BARD proceeds step-by-step through the following chapters. We provide chapter summaries to give you a potent overview of what you will be exposed to in this book.

Chapter Summaries:

Chapter 1: Ballard's Alignment and Reporting Disciplines

Our purpose is to enable Facilitators, CEOs, CFOs, COOs, leaders, and entrepreneurs to guide enterprises toward long-term customer loyalty, achievement of business objectives, and improvement of cash flow from operations. In the Preface, Andy Bargerstock lays out his decades-long search for the Missing Methodology; that is, a systematic way to connect good business planning to consistent execution of performance in providing value to customers. The Missing Methodology calls for examining and defining linkages between operating activities and financial transactions.

Chapter 1 introduces Ballard's Alignment and Reporting Disciplines (BARD), a sequential and step-by-step methodology for waking up the organization to its value-creating activities, and then systematically driving the organization to higher levels of alignment, unanimity, agility, and excellence, with cash flow from operating activities as the key improvement reference point.

The five disciplines are:

1. *Map and Identify*: Map the sequence of value-creating activities (VCAs); identify the total set of disconnects, each linked to a VCA.
2. *Analyze and Project*: Conduct three-bottom-line analysis; create rolling what-if cash flow projections with material assumptions indexed.
3. *Define and Link*: Define key financial drivers and disconnects; develop key performance indicators (KPIs) linking activities and transactions.
4. *Engage and Align*: Engage leaders and staff to drive improvements by aligning on both true core facts and desired outcomes.

5. *Monitor and Report*: Regularly monitor performance in periodic huddles using outcome-driven agendas to generate an enterprise commons for measurement.

Performed first by the CEO, the Reality Check consists of applying the first three disciplines to their personal tacit knowledge about total value creation. Then, the CEO pulls the CFO into the dialogue, and finally the entire senior team is engaged. Learning to effectively align with others happens in Chapters 5 and 6. We tie all the pieces together in Chapters 7 and 8, Value Streams linking to the total Value Cycle, and Boosting Enterprise Performance.

We conclude most chapters with the perspective of Jeff Lueken, the CEO of Lueken's Food Stores, a family-owned grocery chain based in Bemidji, Minnesota. Founded by Joe Lueken in the 1960s, it was Joe, with his wife and sons, who decided to give the enterprise to the 400-person staff, and thereby the community, before his passing. This family's decision was heralded by newspaper headlines, and state and national television coverage. One of Joe's four sons, Jeff Lueken, is overseeing the hand-off to the enterprise Employee Stock Ownership Program leadership. He expresses one senior leader's experience with BARD methods as he prepares his leadership team for effective staff engagement.

We reveal the methods for conducting the CEO Reality Check in the following three chapters.

Chapter 2: Map the Value-Creating Activity Cycle

BARD #1 maps the sequence of value creation by indexing the complete cycle of value-creating activities.
In this chapter, see how to create work products that define both operating activities that create value and the location of critical business problems that interfere with the team's abilities to drive business performance. See actual examples of the work products developed at Maryland Association of CPAs during their Management Operating System Upgrade, facilitated using BARD.

The CEO's draft of the Chart of Activities (CoA) begins the process of defining how value is created by the organization. This initial template functions as the CEO's private reference document for assessing subsequent iterations. The documents evolve through eliciting staff to share their own tacit job knowledge about value creation (before seeing any other person's work on the subject).

The CoA sequences Value-Creating Activities (VCAs) through the four domains of enterprise. The four domains are ordered categories of the value-creating activities sequence:

- Market Segmentation and Prospect Identification
- Customer/Client Acquisition Sequence
- Value Delivery Sequence
- Back Office/Support

Enterprises develop a clear vision of value creation by defining their CoA within a sequence of 19 to 22 value-creating activities. After value-creating activities are defined, they create a visual graphic called the Value Cycle Map, which serves as an evolving one-page institutional document representing "what we do here and order in which we do it." Chapter exhibits show real case examples—development of the CoA and Value Cycle Maps at the Maryland Association of CPAs (MACPA).

At the conclusion, we encourage enterprise leaders to begin building unanimity by first drafting their own Chart of Activities using a drafting template provided as an exhibit, and available upon request at www.businessexpertpress.com/books/mastering-leadership-alignment -linking-value-creation-cash-flow

Chapter 3: Conduct three-bottom-line analysis

BARD #2 offers a whole system view of the enterprise financials

When leaders create a financial "big picture" that everyone understands and feels valued in assessing, whole-hearted unanimity emerges about the core facts of the enterprise. This chapter focuses on how three Bottom Lines give a quick overview of what is happening in the enterprise. To illustrate the basic organization of financial statements and their connections to the three Bottom lines, we provide sample condensed financial statements of a hypothetical company named ZYY Corporation.

You will learn about the different crucial perspectives revealed by monitoring three-bottom-line performance numbers:

- Cash Flow from Operating Activities
- Net Profit
- Return on Assets

Cash Flow from Operating Activities is the first subtotal from the Cash Flow Statement, and is also known as Operating Cash Flow (OCF). We show how to effectively understand this number using the Direct Method of calculation, which is most easily understood by leaders.

Net Profit is calculated based on the accrual concept of accounting, which is required by publicly traded companies. It shows "earned" profits by using a method of realizing revenues and recognizing expenses in a manner that minimizes the potential for misrepresentation. Accrual accounting matches revenues and related expenses, grouped within the same period of time they occur (Month, Quarter, Year).

Return on Assets (ROA) is a ratio of Net Profit divided by Average Total Assets. ROA is a type of return-on-investment calculation. As a key measure for evaluating management effectiveness, ROA gives a percentage of profit returned annually based on assets utilized by a business. ROA is a ratio of Net Profit divided by Average Total Assets. It provides a single overall measure of how well the leadership have performed on their stewardship responsibilities.

In this chapter examples of three basic financial statements are given: Balance Sheet, Income Statement, and Cash Flow Statement.

BARD employs an set of material assumptions to provide a validated and accurate picture of future OCF, especially for the next 90 to 180 days. The exhibits show the approach MACPA took to understand and share this financial "big picture" with leaders, including an innovation called Ballard's Material Assumptions Index (that Ballard was amazed to find does not appear to exist in standard Pro Forma practice).

IBM ROA Graph Example

BARD's Return-on-Assets Map shows the third bottom line and two key financial drivers. It comes with the book. We invite the marketplace to use this ROA Graph at will (and provide a no-fee template to do so), so everyone who needs to can see exactly how well the whole system is creating value over time with the assets it employs, and likely how it will apply its assets in future. MOS Upgrade core methods and technology were pivotal for the first 28 years (upper left) of IBM's 58-year trajectory mapped below.

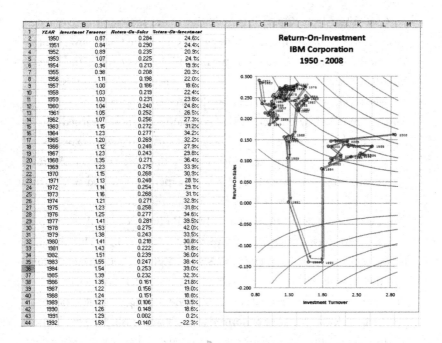

Chapter 4: Link Disconnects and KPIs to Financial Drivers

BARD #3 addresses the question—What is not working as well as it could and how can that be measured in a way that causes the situation to improve? And how should the team approach performance measurement so that unintended consequences are minimal?

The term "disconnects" is used, rather than other terms for problems, because disconnect connotes issues of design, function of the environment, and the whole system, rather than inferring blame on a specific individual, team, or function.

In this chapter, we see how to create behavioral and financial scoreboards to effectively guide enterprise toward greater value creation excellence. We begin by defining the characteristics of Key Performance Indicators (KPIs). We learn about the 10 internal financial drivers that combine mathematically to produce the Three-Bottom-Line Results and how KPIs directly affect one or more of those drivers. In addition, we discover two external financial drivers that are important for bankers and investors in their assessment of enterprise operating health.

Along the way, we focus on discovering how nonfinancial data about value-creating activities can support the progressive enhancement of these metrics. Defining the Cash Conversion Cycle completes the driver's section. Tracking Cash Conversion integrates and aligns all the pieces of enterprise to a laser focus.

We learn how to further refine the Value Cycle Map to show improvement initiatives; discover how to effectively define and validate the three to five most important disconnects and KPIs for monitoring progress to eliminate obstacles to value creation flow; see how MACPA applied Financial Scoreboard to track their financial performance over more than 10 years, and chose the master measures for focus by everyone.

With the CEO (or senior system steward designate) having performed the Reality Check personally, the next step involves engaging other members of the Senior Team.

Chapter 5: Engage and Align leaders, then staff

BARD #4 establishes the foundation for whole-hearted unanimity.
In this chapter, a CEO or the Senior System Steward sees how to take what they learned in the CEO Reality Check (through personal engagement in the first three Ballard disciplines and the document drafts created) to invite and lead senior leaders into discovery of their own knowledge of enterprise value creation and discover how to align enterprise leadership.

BARD shows how to begin the process of achieving ever-widening circles of whole-hearted unanimity. Beginning with the CEO and CFO, they align their thinking about the core facts of the enterprise—its property, its contracts, its cash, and its activities. Then, the CEO and CFO can proceed with confidence to coherently and elegantly model the way for colleagues to join the documentation. The cascading of BARD requires that all persons joining the conversation complete their own tacit knowledge documenting first in writing, just like the CEO and CFO before them, before entering into discussion of collaborative work products on value creation.

The groundwork for any major or minor decision is laid thoroughly by creating a documented measurement policy development and deployment environment, so that when everyone actually gets in the room together, the discussion centers around solidifying alignment rigorously, and on the fine points of actual execution, rather than wasting time on false starts while trying to hammer out a path of action. Documentation more than covers Sarbanes-Oxley requirements.

The exhibits show just how simply this tacit knowledge that has been mined from a group can be presented, using one-page dashboards to reflect back the collective gathering of facts about value creation.

Chapter 6: Monitor and Report Performance

BARD #5 continuously builds upon the whole-hearted unanimity.
In this chapter, we learn how to use regular, effectively run meetings to promote forward momentum toward creating a fully aligned senior leadership team committed to achieving excellence. Kremer's four questions serve as the guiding template for each meeting to establish a sturdy foundation for senior leadership to develop unanimity on fundamental value creation. That unanimity will serve as the basis for working in alignment to discover, establish, and test the organization's most critical KPIs.

After three to five Key Disconnects have been identified, and KPIs have been developed to monitor progress of improvement efforts, the senior team must experiment with effective periodic improvement meetings called "huddles."

Huddle meetings follow the four-question meeting agenda developed by Chuck Kremer:

- Which of the three bottom lines is weakest?
- Which of the key drivers impacts that bottom line?
- What is the business story behind that driver and its effect on the bottom line?
- What are the most important things that need to be corrected?

This chapter shows how to manage expectations emerging from huddle meetings and how to continuously create a sense of responsibility and accountability for implementing improvements.

Straightforward and common-sense tips for managing huddles and progressive improvements also appear in this chapter. The exhibits provided show additional one-page reports that MACPA used with impact teams to support effective collaboration. You will see a revised Value Cycle Map with three high-priority improvement initiatives including relevant KPIs.

When the senior team learns how to huddle, it will build a stronger foundation of whole-hearted unanimity that leads inevitably to more joy at work and a strong basis for wider staff and stakeholder engagement in the unanimity.

Chapter 7: Connecting Value Streams to the Total Value Cycle

This chapter begins by offering an overview of Value Streams, with an example of how they can integrate into an Income Statement. Bargerstock's Value Stream Income Statement illustrates one method to connect activities with the transactions on the P&L they generate.

The Four Domains of BARD's Chart of Activities provide the organizing paradigm for a new version of the Income Statement that reveals sequentially how value-creating activities produce profits and cash flow. This newly available tool puts financial transactions appropriately in the context of the activities that create them in the first place.

Easy-to-understand financial reports linked with activity reports are crucially important for moving toward transforming into a high-performing enterprise, because they assist in effectively monitoring progress to achieve results with new priorities.

BARD's summary Income Statement can be broken into component income statements, one for each product or service line by using Bargerstock's Lean Management Value Stream model. Assigning a large majority of staff as 100 percent dedicated to one product/service level stream attempts to "assign" costs rather than "allocate" costs. Previously treated as common operating costs, staff resources now get assigned to specific teams working full-time to maximize profitability of their value stream. The recast statement highlights other improvement goals such as inventory reductions, scrap, and warranty costs.

The Spinning Wheels Bike Company portrays a composite of methods observed in various enterprises utilizing Lean Accounting methods.

At the conclusion, we again encourage enterprise leaders to begin building unanimity by first drafting their own Chart of Activities using a drafting template provided as an exhibit, and downloadable on the Mastering Leadership Alignment website, if they haven't already. The Chart of Activities provides necessary context for the Chart of Financial Accounts to fully support the Value Cycle.

Chapter 8: Boosting Enterprise Performance

In this concluding chapter, we summarize by reflecting on the usefulness of BARD methods to generate alignment on value creation across the entire enterprise, and to build unanimity on priorities for improving value-creating activities.

The Ballard Method fulfills the criteria for the Missing Methodology described in the introduction of this book. More precisely, the Method lays out systematic, step-by-step procedures for (a) understanding an organization's value-creating activity sequence, (b) discovering the obstacles to flow of resources, (c) streamlining the paths toward frictionless value creation, and (d) continuously monitoring progress and resharpening the focus for business improvement.

Three mini-case studies from Oklahoma Blood Institute, NAPA Auto Parts (Northern CA Franchise), and Indigenous Designs reveal how widely different enterprises flourished with implementing BARD. All three reported a variety of positive business results including meaningful improvements cash flow from operating activities.

A state of flow at work can naturally ensue in the enterprise with everyone crystal clear about one thing: creating value through understanding how their activities directly affect Operating Cash Flow. Among three case enterprises of four million to 68 million dollars of annual Sales Revenue, average Cash Flow from Operating Activities improvement to the bank account balance was $1,019,00 in the first 12 months, representing an average Operating Cash Flow improvement of 79 percent.

In the Appendices, we provide additional actual cases that illustrate the million-dollar impacts BARD had on improved cash flow and profitability, enhancing market share, while also transforming the workplace toward high achievements through staff engagement and enhancing job satisfaction.

BARD Method Elements

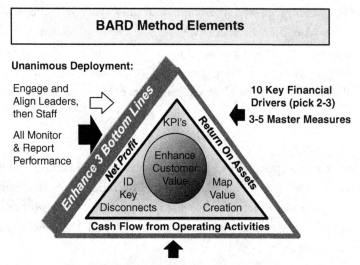

The triangular graphic framing the BARD Method Elements depicts the smooth interplay between the people and the knowledge related to four critical elements: Value Creating Activities, Engaged Staff, 3–5 Master Measures and Three Bottom Lines. The bottom lines (Cash Flow from Operating Activities, Net Profit, and Return on Assets) serve as feedback loops about the effectiveness of the BARD Management Operating System (MOS) upgrade.

Four elements inform improvement impact measurement teams in their work, as they apply the scientific method collaboratively. First, the CEO and/or another Senior Steward drafts value creation maps that include 19–22 Value Creating Activities, beginning to define precisely how the organization delivers value to customers, and also how it generates all its financial outcomes. From this foundation, the CEO aligns with the CFO first, and then the senior team adds their tacit work knowledge to the value creation framework. Whole-heartedly agreeing on the sequence of the current value-creating activities, the senior team can then focus on becoming thoroughly aligned on the entire value creation framework, and candidate master measures. Next, the senior team elegantly invites key people to help them further identify key disconnects (i.e., breakdowns) in value-creating activities. The initial circle of collaborators comes to alignment about 3–5 draft key performance indicators (KPIs) to monitor, that can best assess progress in streamlining and simplifying priority operating activities. Over time the BARD Method then fully engages and integrates people throughout the organization in an adventure of satisfying, if not delighting, customers, satisfying themselves, and steadily improving results as IBM, and more recent MOS Upgrade cases demonstrate conclusively.

Summary

Now are you prepared to dive into applying Ballard's Alignment and Refinement Disciplines as a powerful method for lifting joy of leaders and staff in contributing to enterprise performance? Should you wish to dig into the assumptions underlying BARD, you will find the following great works helpful:

Assumption 1. Existing unanimity about value creation is hidden in financials.

Managing by the Numbers: A Commonsense Guide to Understanding and Using Your Company's Financials, Kremer, Rizzuto & Case, INC/Perseus, 2000.

Assumption 2. CEO and CFO roles have a built-in structure that generates dissonance.

Transforming Performance Measurement: Rethinking the Way We Measure and Drive Organizational Success, Dean Spitzer, AMACOM, 2007.

Accountability: Freedom and Responsibility without Control, Lebow and Spitzer, Berrett Koehler, 2002.

Assumption 3. Alignment begins with Senior Leaders and cascades downwards.

Report from Task Force 1, Unpublished, Hearst, with Ballard, 1983.

Assumption 4. Over 50 percent of enterprise value-creating assets reside in staff job knowledge

Deep Smarts: How to Cultivate and Transfer Enduring Business Wisdom, Leonard & Swap, Harvard Business School Press, 2005.

Assumption 5. Whole-hearted unanimity springs from discovering core objective facts

Beyond IBM, Mobley and Mckeown, McGraw-Hill, 1989.

Why Do A Captain's Reality Check?—Ballard, Scanlon Leadership Network E-Zine, 2008.

Assumption 6. Generally, there is one primary constraint and two to four secondary constraints in a complex work system

Theory of Constraints—*The Goal, Goldratt,* North River Press, 1984 and Systems Thinking.

Assumption 7. Any senior leader with requisite skills can build senior team unanimity

The Art of Focused Conversation: 100 Ways to Access Group Wisdom in the Workplace, Stansfield et al, Canadian Institute of Cultural Affairs, 1997.

CPA Vision Project: Focus on the Horizon—2011 and Beyond, AICPA, 1997.

The technical definition of a KPI emerged from the CPA visioning project in the late 1990s. This initiative on the part of the CPA profession leadership focused on how CPAs can add value for their clients and colleagues.

CHAPTER 1

Ballard's Alignment and Reporting Disciplines

Ballard's Alignment and Reporting Disciplines

1. *Map and Identify*: Map the sequence of VCAs; identify disconnects.
2. *Analyze and Project*: Three-bottom-line analysis with rolling cash flow projections.
3. *Define and Link*: Define financial drivers and disconnects; develop key KPIs linking activities and transactions.
4. *Engage and Align*: Engage leaders and staff by aligning on both true core facts and desired outcomes.
5. *Monitor and Report*: Regularly monitor performance in periodic huddles using outcome-driven agendas.

This primer on enterprise execution intends to enable CEOs, leaders, facilitators, and entrepreneurs to guide their enterprise toward long-term customer loyalty, achievement of business objectives, and improvement of cash flow from operating activities. In the preface and introduction to this book, we laid out the decades-long search for a Holy Grail, or what we call the Missing Methodology, that is, a systematic way to connect good business financial planning to consistently excellent performance in daily operating activities.

Contemporary management pundits speak about the importance of cultivating flexible, adroit thinking and problem-solving skills that can adapt to changing circumstances. Five books provide the backdrop for our adventure on how to systematically build enterprise unanimity with an effective system for closing the business performance gap.

1. In ***Deep Smarts: How to Cultivate and Transfer Enduring Business Wisdom***, Leonard and Swap assert the importance of capturing the vast inherent (tacit) knowledge contained in the hearts, minds, and direct work experience of employees. Up to 50 percent of organizational capital goes undocumented, remaining in the form of tacit knowledge that cannot be easily transferred, or otherwise capitalized. Perhaps the greatest vulnerability in American business today springs from our inability to capture employees' crucial enterprise know-how and sustaining wisdom (Leonard and Swap, 2005). **Our take-away: Leadership and staff engagement and documentation of tacit knowledge are critical to developing wise and efficient ways to improve business performance.**

2. In ***Education: The Discipline of Getting Things Done,*** Bossidy and Charran state, "Execution is not just tactics—it is a discipline and a system. Execution hasn't yet been recognized or taught as a discipline, whereas other disciplines have no shortage of accumulated knowledge, tools and techniques. The leader who executes assembles an architecture of execution" (Bossidy and Charran, 2002. p.28). **Our take-away: Systematic knowledge, tools, and methods provide the discipline and rigor for an architecture of execution.**

3. In the business classic ***Managing by the Numbers*** (Kremer, Rizzuto and Case, 2000), the authors have provided what is apparently the first, and perhaps one of the only books that explains fundamental financial statements with simple common sense, and in plain English. It has sold close to 25,000 copies, largely by word of mouth, as no marketing was ever budgeted for the book after it was published. We will refer to this book throughout as the source guide for the financial side of our Value Creation Framework. **Our take-away: Operational and financial literacy lay the foundation to create feedback and learning loops critical for assessing and monitoring operational progress.**

4. In ***The Art of Focused Conversation (ICA Canada, 1997),*** Stansfield et al. provide 100 ways to access group wisdom in the workplace, and is intended to expand images of what can be accomplished

BALLARD'S ALIGNMENT AND REPORTING DISCIPLINES   3

through the Focused Conversation Method. It demonstrates how many workplace tasks can be accomplished through the medium of focused conversation. Ballard's Alignment and Reporting Disciplines (BARD) is a highly specific form of what is offered in its 25 pages of text and 100 tested agenda designs. BARD methods have been built using this method. **Our take-away: Develop rational and experiential outcomes for meetings first, before agenda setting; and design meetings that start with key data, then explore issues and insights, and end with decision recommendations and next steps.**

5. In *Wheelspin: The Agile Executive's Manifesto*, Mike Richardson refers to organizational agility as the necessary ingredient to address the dynamic complexities of modern business. He refers to the importance of triage as "an acute form of focus, time and priority management in complex situations which are unfolding in real-time with high stakes." Chaos and complexity grow to create a sense of being overwhelmed. Ultimately, "getting organized for agility takes higher order executive strengths" (Richardson, 2011). **Our take-away: Focus and priority management are key ingredients for developing effective systems to deal with complexity profitably.**

Today, as we look back to the evolution of our work in organizational development, we see how key ideas in these books helped shape the development of our guidance to business leaders and community benefit organizations. Gradually, we discovered the various tools needed. Then we crafted an insight-filled line of inquiry, engaging leaders and staff on this path of curiosity about "How well are we actually doing?" Collaboratively documented mining of tacit job knowledge triggers what ultimately can become enterprise-wide alignment and passion for achieving excellence in operating activities.

Ballard's Alignment and Reporting Disciplines

The whole-systems model we use to wake up the enterprise and unlock the genius of its employees is called BARD, five core activities in sequence. BARD consists of integrated elements from value stream analysis, the theory of constraints, metrics-driven culture change, technology of participation, systems thinking, common language development, accountability, preparation and reporting of financials, and lean management.

The five disciplines proceed sequentially in this book.

1. *Map and Identify*: Map the sequence of value-creating activities (VCAs); identify the total set of disconnects, each linked to a VCA.
2. *Analyze and Project*: Conduct three-bottom-line analysis; create rolling what-if cash flow projections with material assumptions defined and indexed.
3. *Define and Link*: Define key financial drivers and disconnects; develop key performance indicators (KPIs) linking activities directly to the cash conversion cycle.
4. *Engage and Align*: Engage leaders and key staff to drive improvements by aligning on both core facts known and agreed to be objectively true, and outcomes to drive.
5. *Monitor and Report*: Regularly monitor performance in periodic huddles using outcome-driven agendas to generate an enterprise commons for mature measurement.

On the basis of decades of experimentation with BARD, we encourage the most senior leader to follow closely this finely tuned path of least resistance toward building a robust sense of unanimity within the organization. Through BARD, discover how to powerfully connect organizaobjectives directly to the day-to-day activities.

First, see how the combination of Value-Creating Activities mapping (VCAs), value chain indexing, and total disconnect analysis provide an accurate and forever repeatable method for continually reprioritizcurrent improvement initiatives across the entire enterprise. This book provides guidance for a precise sequence of leadership self- assessments, each building on the foundation of its previous, easily executed step.

Second, discover concepts and tools to conduct one's own personal bottom lines analysis, and learn how to specify and/or personally generate rolling cash projections without being completely dependent on your valued financial professionals.

Third, learn how to extract the few financial drivers for critical business outcomes, and discover the most useful KPIs we call the 3-5 master measures, some of which will become fully validated key leading indicators over time.

Fourth, you will see how to stimulate high levels of senior leader engagement and alignment that builds and sustains leadership coherence, and then develop key staff capacity for continuously improving both activity and transaction results.

Finally, you will learn methods for self-organizing dialogues among senior, and later, associate leaders, which will keep the entire organization focused and on purpose to achieve continuous results improvements. Upgrades have generated millions of dollars within 12–24 months, as was the outcome in three of the 5 case studies in MLA.

Think of BARD as initiating a management operating system (MOS) upgrade. Some sort of MOS exists currently in every enterprise. The MOS articulates the procedures for activities such as paying employees, paying vendors, and serving customers. However, that existing MOS is almost never documented thoroughly enough for all leaders and eventually line staff, to be unanimously on the same page about all those important things that affect business performance. Through BARD, an enterprise can develop a core of whole-hearted unanimity about its MOS, documented so thoroughly and consistently that the entire business transforms into ever-higher levels of effectiveness.

The bottom lines axiom: **Activity precedes transaction in all cases.**

Unfolding BARD Step by Step

In Chapters 2 to 6, we unfold the five disciplines. In a step-by-step manner, each chapter will show how the development of specific shared and simple work products facilitates progress toward recognizing and addressing those few most important issues. For example, in Chapter 2, where the theme is mapping the value creation sequence, you will learn how to develop a list of 19 to 22 core **Value Creating Activities (VCAs)**. The sequence of value creating activities serves as the foundation for defining a **Chart of Activities (CoA)** that answers the question—What is the sequence of value creating activities we follow to generate satisfied and loyal customers; and all our financial results?

Having a validated CoA permits the development of a draft **Value Cycle Map** about which there will be no arguments because the whole senior team all genuinely had a hand in creating it. After the senior team, and then, prudently, all other staff, get the opportunity to include their value creation insights, this map communicates to everyone a basic picture of how the organization creates value for its customers. It can also be utilized to support and direct discussion about disconnects and waste that are thwarting performance.

Case Study: Maryland Association of CPAs

In most chapters, we demonstrate how each of the disciplines was implemented in a real case situation with a nonprofit professional association, the Maryland Association of Certified Public Accountants (MACPA), one of Jahn Ballard's first clients to experiment with all five disciplines.

Founded in 1901, MACPA had developed a stable brand and mature market when former construction industry CFO, **Tom Hood**, became the new CEO at MACPA in 1996. As a nonprofit organization with 9,000 members and a staff of more than 30 employees, MACPA steadily embraced a mission involving professional education, skills development, and lobbying to help CPAs be successful while protecting the CPA brand. While it is a thriving concern today, in 1996 the MACPA business model was in need of an overhaul. Hood expressed the challenge in this way:

> As senior leaders, all of us have a fundamental challenge with organizational leadership—it is that we're just never done because our businesses are constantly evolving and changing, as are our people. The question then becomes, how do we continually figure the current situation out? How do we engage our people, train them and get them owning our business strategy, and then drive business execution in the right direction?

The problems Tom Hood faced when he arrived included an eroding revenue stream and growing expenses. Much of their revenue came from providing continuing education credits for the state CPA licensing requirements. Yet competitors had entered the market and were offering competing classes, which eroded MACPA revenues. In the past, MACPA had been able to obtain mailing lists of those passing the CPA exam. But new privacy laws prohibited releasing anything other than the names of exam passers. Thus, it had become more complicated to reach newly licensed CPAs. Another observation Tom made was that the organization had a compliance orientation, not a customer value orientation. They had developed a singular tunnel vision that focused on helping members stay compliant with continuing education requirements. Consequently, MACPA was missing opportunities to discover valuable new services that could benefit their membership.

Tom quickly identified the eroding revenue base as a top priority and had some success in reversing the downturn. But, by 2001, Tom wanted to find ways to enlist employees in efforts to further improve organizational performance, as they had grown revenues back over $4 million for that year, while going further into the red, with a negative Cash Flow from Operating Activities of $245,000. So he engaged in collaboration with Jahn Ballard to assist with an initial management system upgrade at MACPA. He started with teaching his staff a three-bottom-line performance view of their association. With this tool and methods, they could all see the financial results they were producing, and easily agree collectively on the few crucial areas for aligned focus of the entire staff. Educating and engaging the whole staff at MACPA in this manner delivered a $971,000 cash flow improvement in the first 12 months, with total revenues of $4 million.

Over the next decade, Ballard visited annually to train CPA members in the Three-Bottom-Line performance as part of their annual Continuing Professional Education credits. Under Hood's and CFO Skip Falatco's leadership and commitment to developing an upgraded operating system, MACPA moved incrementally to improve its business results while providing enhanced value to its membership until 2010. By then, it was clear what was needed was a formal mapping of the value creation sequences so they could be linked more effectively by KPIs to the financial engine. Thus, in the case of MACPA, the three-bottom-line analysis came first, followed later by the mapping of value sequences.

Impact of BARD Intervention at MACPA

In 2014, Tom Hood indicated that, in addition to the first year's $971,000 in new operating cash improvement, MACPA had experienced 12 years of continuing revenue growth and profitability in a mature market through the transparency of shared three-bottom-line accounting. MACPA had average annual revenue growth of 4.3 percent over the previous 12 years in what had appeared initially to be a mature market. After the upgrade, average cash flow from operations rose to $400,000 annually. MACPA was recognized as one of the most innovative nonprofits in the CPA Association industry. Membership satisfaction scores rose significantly as well as membership participation numbers. Many MACPA member firms report 100 percent member participation among their staff professionals.

Sounds impressive, but how did this happen? We reveal the initial phases of progress throughout Chapters 2 to 6, and toward the end of each chapter. As further evidence of the impact of BARD methodology, CEO Jeff Lueken reflects below on the transformation of his family business beginning with the BARD CEO Reality Check.

Jeff Lueken, CEO, Lueken's Food Stores, Reflects on Practical Methodology of BARD

Several years ago my father, an independent grocer of 46 years, expressed his wish to form an ESOP for his business so that it could be left to the communities he served. I had moved away many years prior to pursue my own career. However, since I grew up in the business and fully understood his local focus and people-centric values, he asked that I manage this transition for him. I initially took my traditional path of extensive research. After reading many books on the ESOPs and peripheral subjects, I was led to the book *Managing by the Numbers* and ultimately to Ballard's Alignment and Reporting Disciplines. This Reality Check has been just what I was looking for, because it strikes at the heart of how to involve people meaningfully in the operation of their business.

What attracted me to the CEO Reality Check, which I have not seen in any other offerings, was BARD's focus on both the human element and simple practicality. The approach is flexible, organic, and complete. Documenting such a practical and common sense look at ourselves has given us a better handle on where and who we really are.

Jeff has been a steward of the family legacy, whom it has been a privilege to serve since 2012 both in the Reality Checks, and the MOS

Upgrade integrating KPIs with 30 self-selecting leaders and staff of Lueken's Foods in 2016.

Before we learn a little about the sources of the work herein, this is what you can expect from proper implementation of BARD.

Realistic Benefits from BARD Implementation

- **Improved cash flow from operating activities**
- **Dramatically enhanced employee engagement and morale**
- **Elimination of various forms of waste and inefficiencies**
- **Lower employee turnover**
- **Enhanced customer loyalty and repeat business orders**

Ballard's Early Inspiration and Guidance

Jahn Ballard gives credit to many different mentors who inspired his thinking and shaped the development of BARD. The three most influential and relevant of those mentors were Lou Mobley, Chuck Kremer, and Jack Ballard. Their brief and inspiring stories provide much of the foundational context from which these methods for evoking and documenting wholehearted unanimity on core facts of enterprise have evolved.

Lou Mobley

Lou Mobley (mob-lee), an engineer from Georgia Tech by training, began contributing to financial reporting nearly 50 years ago, with his creation of the Return-on-Asset Stewardship (ROA) Chart.[1] His ROA visualization tool was the basis for discussions with DuPont's Treasurer, who made the Du Pont Formula public at the American Management Association in 1952. Starting in 1955, Lou was on the staff that founded and was a Director at IBM's Sands Point Executive School, doing executive development for IBM's Tom Watson Jr. Lou invented the ROA Chart to illustrate to DuPont's Treasurer that ROA generated deeper insights when it was broken down into component ratios as Return on Sales times Asset Turnover. Despite Lou's important realization, it did not connect with the treasurer. In time Lou's ROA breakdown became part of university finance

---

[1] Available at http://integralpmi.com/accounting-30--case-studies/ibm-roi-case.html.

textbooks and public reporting of financials on Wall Street. Lou decided to support his student executives in implementing what was known as the Profit Planning initiative in 1957, using the ROA Chart. This and other simple analysis tools gave IBM's executive leadership resources to drive their global ascendancy over the next 30 years to become the most successful and best-managed enterprise ever seen in the world up until that time. See IBM case synopsis in the Appendices for a one-page view of its history from 1950 to 2008, using Mobley's Return on Asset Stewardship Chart.

Lou discovered his legendary "Mobley Matrix" as IBM execs dubbed it, in 1959, and later created a software version with his son Chris, which was introduced to the US market by Jahn Ballard in 1986. Its forward-looking projection capabilities made it the most sophisticated, simplest, and fastest modeling and forecasting tool for financial statement the US market had seen to date. One of the reasons for that achievement was its clear disclosure of three sources of cash flows—from Operating, Financing, and Investing Activities, and its ability to accurately project those flows into the future. Ballard learned, tested, priced, and sold the first Mobley Matrix software licenses into the market on both the East and the West Coasts in 1986.

The following year FASB reg. 95 made cash flow reporting mandatory due to Mobley's successful 7-year letter writing campaign to demand a Cash Flow Statement to accompany Balance Sheets and Income Statements in Generally Accecpted Accounting Principles (GAAP), so entrepreneurs could develop command of their cash.

Chuck Kremer

Beginning in 1984 with Lou Mobley's introduction, Jahn Ballard enjoyed both a personal and professional relationship with Chuck Kremer, creator of Financial Scoreboard®, and author of *Managing by the Numbers* (Kremer et al., 2000). Ballard spent many years refining and extending Mobley and Kremer's innovative concepts related to three-bottom-line performance and management. In so doing, he determined that there were missing elements needed to provide the required guidance to drive each of the bottom lines.

Mobley and Kremer identified the three bottom lines and 12 key financial drivers as important high-altitude feedback tools. Ballard discovered that a small set of nonfinancial numbers drive financial results, and that leaders and staff know what they are if asked politely and sincerely, and given a fair chance to think things through together. So with Kremer's support after Mobley passed away in the late 1980s, Ballard has focused for decades on demonstrating methods that enable the senior team to be able to examine how the enterprise creates value for customers, where, specifically, the value chain breaks down, and how to continuously repair and improve business processes—all with direct linkage to the financials if required or desired. With the new insights gained from years of BARD development and while continuing to leverage Kremer's great contributions, Ballard saw in client partnerships a consistent improvement in cash flow from operating activities, along with a concurrent boost to employee satisfaction and job tenure.

Jack Ballard

Around 1970, Jack Ballard, having been in international finance since 1956, was Director of Personnel for a Fortune 50 company's international division, responsible for over 3,000 executives in more than 100 countries. He was also Executive Committee Chair at Wainwright House: Center for the Development of Human Resources. His least favorite activity at work was making the weekly personnel report to the executive committee. The board table became a global board game with his executive charges as the chess pieces. One day he changed the name of the Executive Committee's agenda item to the Human Resources Report. He interspersed his report with profiles of specific people and their families across the globe, so no one could forget that these were people they were discussing. He later changed the title on his card to Director of Human Resources, and began to systematically create ways for all those people to have the highest possible levels of satisfaction personally, while being highly productive and growing in their jobs as well. Bosses became trained mentors and coaches to all their direct reports, possibly for the first time ever in a Fortune 50 scale company.

With mentorship from Lou Mobley at IBM and Robert Greenleaf at AT&T/Bell Labs, Jack mastered the art of what he called "nondirective leadership," in which one avoids answering questions directly, but rather uses the Socratic Method of answering a question by posing another question that allows the person to discover their own truth. Nondirective leaders aspire to never tell people what they should do; instead, they help others to discover what to do next. BARD takes it further, recommending that new policy proposals come from a team, with a clear intent statement and defined outcomes.

As the first executive in a Fortune 50 company to have the title Director of Human Resources, Jahn Ballard's father, Jack, provided an early foundation for the corporate human resources profession in American business. He based his approach on the principle that productive and satisfied people who are fully informed will naturally create the highest possible value wherever they are. He created large-scale cultural change by enabling leaders to discover their purpose and passion, and to learn how to give their gifts without coercion. His father was deeply committed to understanding the worlds in which he lived and worked, and learning how to build organizational capacity to care more effectively for people. He especially focused on developing the ability to discover, direct, and manifest our own destiny as individuals, as expressed by our natural genius, and to care effectively for those closest to us.

When Jahn was struggling to find an effective direction for implementing Mobley and Kremer's breakthroughs, it was Jack who pointed him in the direction of focus on the nonfinancial measures, the operating activity data that creates all financial outcome data. With that simple insight, Ballard was able to begin systematically drawing out and recording people's knowledge and measures of their nonfinancial world, and then help them to see how those nonfinancial numbers drove all the numbers in their financial world.

The bottom lines insight: **Activity precedes transaction in all cases.**

Management Operating System (MOS) Upgrade

Through implementing an MOS Upgrade (www.mosupgrade.com), Ballard's client partners' KPI and Decision teams have utilized BARD methods to produce significant business improvements for manufacturing, service, and community benefit enterprises. As we develop the full model of BARD in this book, we will refer to an array of no-fee supplementary materials available at www.MOSupgrade.com/MLA/Library.

With this overview, we are now ready to see how to explore and directly experience the five disciplines.

References

Kremer, C., Rizzuto, R., and Case, J. (2000). *Managing by the Numbers: A Commonsense Guide to Understanding and Using Your Company's Financials.* Cambridge, MA: Inc/Perseus.

Leonard, D., and Swap, W. (2005). *Deep Smarts: How to Cultivate and Transfer Enduring Business Wisdom.* Boston, MA: Harvard Business School Publishing.

Bossidy, L., and Charran, R. (2002). *Education: The Discipline of Getting Things Done.* New York, NY: Crown Business.

Richardson, M. (2011). *Wheelspin: The Agile Executive's Manifesto.* Tempe, AZ: No Limit Publishing Group.

Stansfield et al. (1997). *The Art of Focused Conversation.* Toronto, ON, Canada: ICA.

CHAPTER 2

Mapping the Value-Creating Activities Cycle

Ballard's Alignment and Reporting Disciplines (BARD)

1. *Map and Identify*: Map the sequence of VCAs; identify disconnects.
2. *Analyze and Project*: Three-bottom-line analysis with rolling cash flow projections.
3. *Define and Link*: Define financial drivers and disconnects; develop key KPIs linking activities and transactions.
4. *Engage and Align*: Engage leaders and staff by aligning on both true core facts and desired outcomes.
5. *Monitor and Report*: Regularly monitor performance in periodic huddles using outcome-driven agendas.

In this chapter, learn how to create three aligned work products that will result in defining both your operating activities that create value and the location of critical business problems that interfere with your team's ability to drive business performance. You will see actual examples of the work products developed at Maryland Association of Certified Public Accountants (MACPA) during their Management Operating System Upgrade facilitated by Jahn Ballard using BARD.

The three BARD work products for this chapter are:

- **Value-Creating Activities (VCAs) sequence organized as a numbered Chart of Activities (CoA)**
- **Disconnects List brainstorm**
- **Value Cycle Map first draft**

Managing business alignment through BARD begins with drafting the Value-Creating Activities cycle.

BARD is a method to create an ongoing "focus group" internally with the senior team about how the enterprise serves its internal customers, who then create value for the external customers. Drafting and ongoing refinement of the CoA is a primary collaborative work product, with improvement priorities more sharply defined by documenting where value is flowing unimpeded to the end customer, and where it is not flowing unimpeded. After the "big picture" is unanimous among the senior team, then sensitive and effective engagement of all key stakeholders has track to run on. When, after some months of working with the new practices, the senior team gets anchored solidly in unanimity on the VCAs and where they are breaking down, key staff can be invited with great care into the collaborative value-design process.

Moving into the CEO's Reality Check

If there is a need to improve business execution, this suggests there are constraints (disconnects) in the processes used to create products or services. Beyond possible disconnects in business process design, there may also be behavioral constraints coming from the activities performed by employees. We usually find disconnects in the handoffs between **both** business processes utilized and in the behaviors of the people using those processes.

Many organizational development initiatives fail early because of insufficient preparation, leading to a less-grounded commitment of either the CEO and/or other Senior System Stewards. With BARD, failure is avoided by establishing the proper tone at the top through thoughtful and patient preparation. Usually, it is the CEO who leads the way, often with the support of a coach with strong facilitation skills. Sometimes a CFO or some other Senior System Steward takes the first drafting role. For the sake of illustration, we will assume it is the CEO leading the way.

The CEO Reality Check consists of the steps revealed in Chapters 2 to 4. In this process, the CEO's "enduring wisdom" or "tacit knowledge" reveals enterprise assets that were present before to the CEO, but not recorded for knowledge transfer. These phrases refer to the inherent and most often hidden knowledge of the enterprise that lies dormant within the brain of all staff, often found to be more concentrated within the senior team because of their broad responsibilities and experience depth.

This is a necessary precursor to collaboration with others. When a senior leader has explored comprehensively their own view of the business system, they are then in a position to draw out the tacit knowledge of others in a way that does not manipulate or distort the new input. Simultaneously, the CEO gains leadership stature for guiding the senior management team collaboratively toward unanimity. This is the foundation for meaningful discussion and clarification of the current state of the enterprise's true condition.

Exhibit 2A on p.115 illustrates the cascading path of BARD. Three concentric circles represent the ever-widening tacit knowledge documentation effects. Begin with the CEO's Reality Check (1), which when aligned with the CFO (2), becomes the foundation to engage the Senior Team (3). Then eventually, once written and whole-hearted unanimity is present in the senior team, it is cascaded to key stakeholders at large (4).

There are times in enterprise when people appear to be in conflict among themselves as they try to figure out what they think about various situations. People seek a complete set of facts as a reference point for thinking things through. Often what appears to be communication conflict is really a process of each staff member gathering enough information to figure out where they stand, so they may converse intelligently and with relevance. When the CEO articulates her or his own personal tacit knowledge on enterprise value creation to him or herself, the groundwork is established to lead the next level of leadership each on their own personal self-discovery and internal dialogue about VCAs. The CEO can then lead their team through any stormy seas to build consensus and points of unanimity. We will examine how to engage the senior team step by step through BARD in Chapter 5.

Begin with the short definition of enterprise mission. If you already have a formal mission statement, that enterprise artifact is the place to start. We remind ourselves of the intended collective purpose of our culture. If there has not been a formal mission statement, then create one sentence as a working draft for the purpose of this exercise. Later, this draft can be useful to gain alignment about enterprise common purpose. A mission statement is often a one-sentence statement of the fundamental purpose of being in the marketplace—typically in terms of whom we serve, what we provide, and how we provide it.

To effectively guide an organization toward achieving more of what has been planned, CEOs and senior leaders need to understand deeply how value creation emerges from the operating activities performed. These operating activities lead to and create all financial transactions. Some activities create value, and some destroy value. To work with clarity toward finding the root causes of value destruction, we each need to understand how the value-creating processes unfold in the enterprise. The CEO or other Senior Steward has to go there first to map out the territory.

BARD #1: Map the VCAs Cycle emerges by following three steps described below. The CEO (or other Senior System Steward) begins the process that we call the Reality Check. After the senior leader develops their own observations and personal documents, then that leader is best prepared to bring others into the conversation on organizational transformation through BARD. Whoever plays the role of Senior System Steward never shares their personal work products until after another has shared their insight as notes or in writing, in order to ensure that the tacit knowledge of the next collaborator is not distorted before they can share it, and their input is included.

Step 1: Defining VCAs

The CEO Reality Check begins by developing a list of VCAs (normally somewhere between 19 and 21 value creation accounts) that defines the full cycle of value creation in the enterprise.

The Focus Question: "What is the sequence of value-creating activities we follow to generate a satisfied and loyal customer/client, and that produces all our financial results?"

Four domains of VCAs:
- Market Segmentation and Prospect Identification
- Customer/Client Acquisition Sequence

- Customer/Client Value Delivery Sequence
- Back Office Support Activities

The target number, after refinement, is to define 19 to 22 major VCA arenas. These 19 to 22 VCA Accounts become a numbered index for all the rest of the individual value chains in the enterprise. These numbered VCA Accounts can also be used to link activities to the Chart of (Financial) Accounts and/or the General Ledger so an activity-to-transaction linkage is established and defined.

The initial questions/statements to begin development of each of the four VCA lists:
- How do we segment our market and identify prospects?
- Define the sequence normally followed to convert prospects into customers.
- Describe the activities for delivering value to our customers.
- Identify how back office operations provide critical support for the value creation cycle.

We provide several exhibits as examples of the development of the VCA documents.
- Exhibit 2B on p.116 is a template for brainstorming the activities that lie within each of the above four domain. If you want to create a working copy of this template, then allow for more lines beyond the three provided. At least five to seven activities in each domain are ideal for this first pass. A CoA drafting template can be requested from www.MOSupgrade.com/MLA/Library .
- Exhibit 2C on p.117 shows the CFO and CEO's first draft CoA that evolved from the initial brainstorming done utilizing the 2B template. This provided a draft for the left-column information for Exhibit 2D, where the newly drafted VCAs are shown next to the perceived breakdowns (disconnects) in those activities.
- Exhibit 2D on p.118 shows the refined version of activities and disconnects after input was received from all senior team members. This is a partial view of the entire document.

MACPA's Example of VCAs

MACPA was an organization that was struggling to build membership at a time when the available target audience of CPAs in the State of Maryland appeared to be a mature market. Everyone at MACPA was challenged to think creatively about how membership could be expanded. The dynamic insights of the group work that came from the upgrade provided the opportunity to explore where the assumptions or opportunities were blocking the ability to harvest new members.

EXAMPLE: Notice item #5 in the list on 2D. In the process of developing this work product, some new ideas emerged for adding new services to address the need for "second life" training including opportunities to add value with technology training or advanced training in the tools that accountants use. An innovative training program might attract nonmembers and open the door to messaging about the advantages of MACPA membership.

Step 2: Identifying Disconnects in the Enterprise VCAs

Step back and ask what are the three to four most significant problems currently faced by the enterprise. Start with the one that may be keeping you as the CEO awake at night. This question denotes a big picture view in which the CoA draft illustrates how to identify where problems start impacting the flow of VCAs by numbering. Consider and document disconnects for each value creation account. At least one for each number. This documentation process begins to uncover all key disconnects, that is, breakdowns and constraints in business processes.

When Documenting Disconnects

Refine the expression of any breakdown/issue/disconnect until it is expressed as simply as possible in the form of a semantically positive statement of the problem. Here are some examples of positive statement of disconnects identified:

- Research costs for specific waste reduction methods are not budgeted.
- Excessive waiting time (poor production flow) reduces productivity.

- Machine setup times are over 20 minutes, so required minimum batch sizes generate excess inventory.
- Long customer service waiting times significantly lower repeat customers.

After deciding on the draft 19–22 primary VCA Accounts in the four domains, use that list to trigger brainstorming at least one, if not more, disconnects, for each VCA.

Then the question becomes "How do we develop a list of priorities among the list of 30 to 60 disconnects on the list?" or "Which of these 'constraints' to value creation is most easily fixed for the least amount of investment and the greatest amount of return on that investment?" Hold that thought.

We will revisit this question to resolve it in Chapter 4 as we define key financial drivers and key performance indicators (KPIs).

Step 3: The Value Cycle Map—Replacing the Org Chart with an Activities Map

When we create value, customers are happy to pay us for products and services. And if they are delighted with products and services, they send others and come back again and again to buy more.

The Value Cycle Map portrays the value-creating sequence, that is, the major steps from start to finish to create and deliver customer value. We display the sequence as a cycle beginning at the top and moving all the way around in clockwise fashion, only to begin again.

See MACPA's Value Cycle Map (Exhibit 2E on p.119). This sequence of step-by-step VCAs shows how the enterprise addresses the needs expressed by customers for products and services. It begins by "defining customers" and proceeds through all the VCAs that culminate in back office functions that hold the activities together, enabling the cycle to begin again and again.

Notice that in the upper right corner, there is a breakdown of the VCA, Engage Potential Members. The shown content of KPIs and drivers emerged as a co-creation of 30 collaborating staff members in a 2 hour session.

The purpose of the map is to visually and mentally align everyone in the enterprise (who has given written input) with the need to continuously discover the most effective processes for supporting customers' needs, desires, the mission, and mandates.

A fully validated Value Cycle Map can eventually become the visual touchstone for every enterprise conversation that takes place. It can become a primary reference image that organizes framing and coherence of every meeting. Problem-solving processes and activity occur within a resilient context provided by unanimous agreement. The map becomes the visual equivalent of the statement "This is what we do here," and directs the accounting system to be more highly valued by staff because of its relevance to their own activities.

Reflecting on MACPA's approach to giving to each employee a laminated copy of the Value Cycle Map they helped to create, starting from the senior team drafts, Hood stated:

> Having this unanimously affirmed visual reference point brings fantastic clarity and focus to every conversation, because everyone at all levels can see how their areas connect with all the others. They also have greater clarity on both the hand-offs they receive and the ones they make, so the value throughput to our members is as focused, smooth and full of impact as we can make it.

In an enterprise's work with BARD, even though the CEO develops the first version of the map, input from the senior management team will later help refine and align it iteratively. Then, broader engagement of staff can come in due course to "validate" successive versions. Validation occurs when a group has achieved unanimity on a collaboratively evolved Value Cycle Map into which they have all had input.

MACPA Value Cycle Map

For many at MACPA, the Value Cycle Map showed for the first time the full range of services offered by the organization. After the full staff engagement process was completed, the map became an important institutional asset because it showed clearly what MACPA does and the order in which it is done.

Assessing Customer Perspectives of Value

Direct feedback from external customers is critical to understanding how well the VCAs of any enterprise are delivered. Many companies overlook this important step before they engage in improving their business processes and thereby miss a critical opportunity for gaining clarity. Historically, this dialogue has been best accomplished by *focus groups*, where a demographic cross-section of customers meet with a trained facilitator to help them express what's important in final products they purchase.

Reflections on CEO Mapping of VCAs

After the CEO has filled in the complete picture of the facts, at least two things happen. First, the CEO is much clearer and/or dissatisfied with their knowledge levels in specific areas of business operations. Second, the CEO begins to gain clarity about what needs to be done and who needs to get involved. In Chapter 5, we demonstrate how to bridge from the CEO's singular activity to engagement of the senior team.

The Chart of VCAs sets the context for exploring the activities that ultimately drive all the enterprise's financial transactions. Financial statements and reports are like looking out the rear window of a car. They report the history of what has already happened. In effect, financial reports are lagging indicators with respect to predicting the future. In Chapter 4, we will explore more precisely the ratios and relationships that can serve the enterprise as a touchpoint, monitoring progress toward more realistic and precise future financial projections.

Later, in Chapter 6, we will explore an expanded version of the Value Cycle Map after it has been modified to include the three to five most important process improvement measures.

In this chapter, we discovered that the CoA provides the index of all the operating activities, as well as the value creation sequence within each of the VCA accounts. We also learned that the daily behaviors are leading indicators of future results, and that give rise to all financial transactions. Within the 19 to 21 primary VCAs, each activity should have a corresponding named account to accumulate costs in the accounting system. The accounting for value streams will be addressed further in Chapter 7.

At this point, as the CEO or Senior System Steward, you have created a first draft of BARD documents. Do not show your work yet to anyone. There is more work to do before we begin to pull your senior management team members into the adventure. When communicated at the right time, the work done by a prior group is easily transferred to the next level in a nondirective way.

Jeff Lueken, CEO, Lueken's Food Stores, Reflects on His Reality Check

Many of our people said they understood how our business works. However, when I asked them questions, the answers did not come out as quickly as one would think. I would say that was probably even true for me. The Reality Checks's carefully crafted questions gave me pause, caused me to dig deeper and evoked more meaningful answers from both myself and my colleagues.

Now that we, myself, and the current leaders of the ESOP, have completed our Reality Checks, it is easier for us as the leadership group to align on where we are now and where we want to go. It cuts through the noise and gets to the heart of the matter. BARD better assures the ultimate success of making the business sustainable without my father's leadership, and continuing in its culture congruent to my father's values.

In the next chapter, we introduce three-bottom-line performance as the comprehensive tool to use with the Value Cycle Map and Disconnects for evaluating the impact of activities on key performance measures.

CHAPTER 3

Conducting Three-Bottom-Line Analysis

Ballard's Alignment and Reporting Disciplines

1. *Map and Identify*: Map the sequence of VCAs; identify disconnects.
2. *Analyze and Project*: Three-bottom-line analysis with rolling cash flow projections.
3. *Define and Link*: Define financial drivers and disconnects; develop key KPIs linking activities and transactions.
4. *Engage and Align*: Engage leaders and staff by aligning on both true core facts and desired outcomes.
5. *Monitor and Report*: Regularly monitor performance in periodic huddles using outcome-driven agendas.

We will now add another layer to the CEO Reality Check. This chapter focuses on the how Three-Bottom-Line Performance gives a quick and useful overview of what is happening in the enterprise financially. To illustrate the basic organization of financial statements and their connections to the three bottom lines, we provide sample condensed financial statements of a hypothetical company named ZYY Corporation.

In Chapter 5 we will show how the CEO's Reality Check documents provide a foundation for engagement of senior leadership.

According to Chuck Kremer, CPA, many business people do not really use financial information because it is generally presented in financial fragments. The dots are not connected, and so the cause-and-effect relationships are not obvious. The distinction between profits and cash flow is not clear. There is no obvious bottom line for either the cash-flow statement or for the balance sheet. What data is needed for decision-making is not clear. There is no one-page executive summary. Frequently, multi-year trends and ratio analysis are missing. Frequently ratios are missing.

There is no financial glossary. Think about the word "capital" and the 10 ways it can be used with financial statement information (including the term "capital punishment"). There is no story to go with the numbers, which makes the numbers dry, dull, and boring. There is no regular group action planning (huddling) around the numbers. The information is generally presented in a detailed left-brain format, and without summarization. Many people are given the information without the training needed for using the information.

So why is this such a big deal, if lots of business people manage business without paying much attention to their financial statements? Because that is like running the Grand Canyon (or Indy 500) with only one arm or one eye. They may do okay in good economic times because they are very strong in a particular function of their business. But it is difficult to survive and thrive in bad times if you are handicapped in financial literacy. It is difficult to make money over the long term in business if making money is not a focus.

In the book *Managing by the Numbers,* with John Case and Ron Rizzuto, Chuck Kremer provides the basic foundation for using financial statement information to focus rigorously and comprehensively on making money. When coupled with the Ballard Method of Five Alignment Disciplines, both halves of the coin are present for making accounting a science of collaboration, practical accountability, and team-building.

The Three-Bottom-Line Metrics

Virtually, all economic enterprises can be evaluated from a big picture perspective by looking at three calculated numbers from the financial statements: Cash Flow from Operating Activities, Net Profit, and Return on Asset (ROA). Ballard first encountered these metrics when he was introduced to Chuck Kremer in 1984 by Lou Mobley, discoverer of the Three Bottom Lines. *Managing by the Numbers* (Kremer et al., 2000) revealed Mobley's insights to the US market in terms of Generally Accepted Accounting Principles (GAAP). See Exhibit 3A on p.120 for a list of the three bottom lines, how they are calculated, and what they mean for assessing progress.

BOTTOM LINE #1—Cash Flow from Operating Activities (a.k.a. value-creating activities)
BOTTOM LINE #2—Net Profit
BOTTOM LINE #3—Return on Asset Stewardship

Let us dig a little deeper into each of the bottom lines.

1. BOTTOM LINE #1: Cash Flow from Operating Activities

Cash flows are crucial for running any business. The purpose of the Cash Flow Statement is to explain how the bank account has changed in any given period. United States GAAP requires the development of a Cash Flow Statement with three sections: Cash from/to Operating Activities, Cash from/to Investing Activities, and Cash from/to Financing Activities.

Essentially, the Cash Flow Statement creates three buckets into which all the cash-in and cash-out transactions can be placed:

- **Operating activities** involve all value-creating activities serving internal or external customers/clients, and all value-destroying activities as well.
- **Investing activities** involve cash transactions for buying and selling of long-term assets such as a plant, property, and equipment and also marketable securities (short-term investments of idle cash). These are not surplus-related transactions, but rather they are related to building business capacity.
- **Financing activities** involve cash transactions to expand/ retire debt, selling or buying back capital stock, and the payment of dividends. These are not surplus-related transactions; they relate to the combination of debt/equity financing tactics utilized.

Every transaction involving the increase or decrease to cash falls into one of these three categories.

Of the three "buckets" of cash flow activities, the one that reigns supreme in importance is Cash from Operating Activities. For an organization to sustain itself long-term, this number must be positive and ideally growing as fast, or faster, than profit.

Prior to 1987, there was no standard accounting presentation of how the cash dynamics in the bank account actually functioned in a business or enterprise. Lou Mobley contributed to the discipline of Accounting and to the GAAP by driving the creation and adoption in 1987 of FASB 95, an official rule from the Financial Accounting and Standard Board. FASB reg. 95 encourages companies to use the Direct Method of preparing the Cash Flow Statement. It requires portraying the Cash Flow from Operations using the Indirect Method. Unfortunately, the Indirect Method has been the method of choice used by audit firms to prepare the Cash Flow Statement for their clients, as it is required, where the direct method is currently not required.

According to FASB 95, if the Direct Method is selected, then a separate schedule is required that will reconcile Net Income and Net Cash Flow from Operating Activities (Indirect Method).

Either cash flow reporting method will generate the same amount shown for Cash Flow from Operating Activities, known as the first bottom line, because it shows the internal generation of cash from surplus-generating activities. Essentially, this number is cash-basis net surplus instead of accrual-basis net profit (surplus). Operating Cash Flow (OCF) also represents the only objectively factual bottom line because it can be traced to changes in cash accounts. Accordingly, from a management perspective the Direct Method is the useful one for decision makers because it shows the sources and uses of cash created from surplus-generating activities.

The Direct Format Cash Flow Statement was discovered by Lou Mobley at IBM's Sand Point Executive School in 1959, and subsequently approved as a formal accounting document, FASB 95 in November of 1987. The Direct Method is the only cash statement format that presents the actual cash accounts that make up Operating Cash Flow (OCF: aka Cash Flow from Operating Activities). The vast majority of enterprises use the Indirect Format, which cannot clearly show the sources and uses of cash. Based on our review of the literature and our own observations, we estimate less than 2 percent of companies use the Direct Format. In Ballard's personal discussions with Chuck Kremer, Kremer indicated that in his experience, small- to medium-sized businesses significantly underperform in cash flow generation by wasting 25 to 33 percent of OCF potential daily. By Kremer's observations, the people leading the work in companies do not understand the cash flow impacts of their daily decisions and actions.

Ballard's Alignment and Reporting Disciplines (BARD) method leads to improvements in cash flow from operating activities because this is where the impact of activity changes can show up dramatically, even in the first year. When properly implemented, BARD leads to streamlining of operations, eliminating waste, and strengthening the critical steps and hand-offs in value-creating activities. Improved cash flow follows such initiatives.

Many leaders struggle with understanding the Cash Flow Statement because it is usually developed according to the Indirect Method (as shown in Exhibit 3D on p.122). The adjustments of Net Income to determine Cash Flow from Operating Activities strike most people as a puzzle.

Cash Flow from Operating Activities (Indirect Method)

Closely examine the first section called Cash Flow from Operating Activities with the Indirect Method. You will find that there are no cash-related descriptions above the subtotal. Instead there are only accrual items that adjust Net Income to reconcile with cash.

In the Indirect Method, the calculation begins with Net Income. Only after conducting a long series of adjustments does the calculation of Cash from Operating Activities finally emerge. Many leaders and staff understandably end up scratching their heads trying to understand the math. Even some professionally trained accountants need to think carefully about how to accomplish this calculation, let alone bring relevance to the numbers. In college accounting classes, professors tend to spend considerable time on the Indirect Method because it is a GAAP requirement.

Unfortunately, the Indirect Method does not provide leaders and key staff with the kind of information that will help inform them to understand better where they are making the most progress and where they need to improve. Professionally trained accountants often overlook the advantages to their internal customers that could come with defining a more direct and clear path to understanding cash. We prefer the alternative Direct Method.

Cash Flow from Operating Activities (Direct Method)

The Direct Method for preparation of the Cash Flow Statement (Exhibit 3E on p.123) is much more straightforward and understandable. Notice in this exhibit for ZYY Corporation, one can clearly see the categories of expenditures of cash to support revenue-generating activities, that is, purchases of inventory, payments to employees for payroll, and payments of various operating expenses.

How does the Direct Cash Statement compare with the Income Statement? For an enterprise to survive, it must produce positive cash flow from operations. Additionally, as enterprises mature, they may generate 10 to 40 percent higher cash from operations compared to the Net Income reported on the Income Statement. Cash Flow from Operating Activities reveals the sustaining and value-creating power of the enterprise.

Ask if your accountant is preparing the Cash Flow Statement using the Indirect or the Direct Method. Require your financial team to prepare the Direct Method Cash Flow Statement as an auxiliary report.

For an enterprise to be sustainable, it must produce positive cash flow from operations. In our experience, a healthy company should plan to grow its cash flow by about 10 percent annually in concert with a similar Profit growth, after it is established and functioning well. If an enterprise is doing serious work in improving its value cycle effectiveness, the fruits of these actions will inevitably (usually sooner than later) be seen in Cash provided by Operating Activities. Companies that last many decades see to it that OCF growth consistently exceeds Profit growth.

2. BOTTOM LINE #2: Net Profit

Net Profit or Net Income defines the enterprise's traditional view of its bottom line. Because many people are confused about how accounting systems work, it is important to gain some perspective about how the numbers on an Income Statement are recorded in the accounting records.

In Exhibit 3B on p.120 you will find an Income Statement for ZYY Corporation. Net Income is the difference between revenues and expenses. Many people think the income statement is a cash basis report where revenues come from "cash in" and expenses are based on "cash out." However, GAAP require a different recording method for realizing revenues and recognizing expenses. It is called accrual accounting. Let us peel open the mystery of accrual accounting.

Accrual Accounting

In accrual accounting, revenues are recorded when a product or service has been provided even if the revenues are not yet collected (normally because of customer credit agreements). For example, if an enterprise sells a product to a customer on credit, and the inventory is removed from your warehouse, the earnings process is completed and the revenue should be recorded on your books even though the customer will make payment some time later, perhaps 30 to 60 days later. And, expenses are recognized when the expense has been incurred even if not yet paid. For example, if your organization's electric utility meter is read by the meter reader on the 30th of each month and you receive the bill 10 days later, then the utility bill received around January 10 is actually an expense of December. Accountants and auditors learn to look for proper cutoffs so that all the expenses are captured and recorded in the proper month and year. This is what is known as "matching" of revenues and expenses. According to GAAP, this is the best method of assessing an enterprise's true profitability.

With the alternative of cash basis accounting, profits can be manipulated too easily. Assume that you own a company with a 12/31 year-end that uses non-GAAP cash basis accounting and that your CEO year-end bonus and bonus for the CFO is based on "profits" shown on the books. In early December, the CEO and the CFO develop an informal agreement that will increase the possibility that bonuses will be earned. Here is the plan. All revenues will be recorded as cash comes in, but the accounts payable team is instructed to delay payments of most bills until early January. Thus, all the revenues in December have virtually no expenses matched against them. Profit target for the year is achieved and bonuses paid leaving the unpaid bills as a challenge for next year's profitability plan.

Obviously, any "ethical" manager would not do this. In an accrual accounting system, such misrepresentation of the profits would not occur. It is a generally accepted notion that accrual accounting provides the best measure of profitability, even though investors, creditors, leaders, and staff also need the story about cash flow.

In Exhibit 3B, we show the condensed Income Statement for ZYY Corporation for 2015. This statement shows two columns, one for dollars and the second column reveals the percentage relationships of each line as a percentage of Sales Revenue. Thus, Sales Revenue is shown as 100 percent. When you see Cost of Goods Sold in any income statement, you know the company is either a merchandiser (selling inventory as wholesaler or retailer) or a manufacturer. Gross Profit is the difference between Sales Revenue and Cost of Goods Sold. Managers watch gross profit very carefully. This is a number that will be affected by a variety of factors including changing costs of inventory acquisition, labor rates if a manufacturing enterprise, and product markup procedures.

Notice that the Net Income as a percentage of Sales Revenues is 10 percent for ZYY Corporation. This calculation is also known as Return on Sales (ROS), a measure we will explore more thoroughly in Chapter 4.

3. **BOTTOM LINE #3: Return on Asset Stewardship (ROA) = Net Income/Average Total Assets**

   "How much profit was made from total available resources?"

   Return on Assets is Net Income divided by Average Total Assets which is derived by adding the current year's and previous year's Total Assets and dividing by 2. On the balance sheet, assets are mostly valued at depreciated (if applicable) historic cost, not fair market value. The Net Income is based on the accrual accounting definitions for profit-making transactions. Thus, ROA shows the current year's Net Income as a percentage of the historic cost of assets used in the business. ROA will vary from industry to industry but rarely exceeds 15 to 20 percent.

Some financial analysts will use Operating Income (before deductions of interest expense and taxes) instead of Net Income. So, if you are comparing your organization's ROA to industry averages, be sure to also find data on both ROS and Asset Turnover (ATO), which are the multiplied components of Mobley's view of ROA. Industry associations often collect such data from member organizations. For publicly traded companies, industry averages for ROS and ROA can be found in a variety of investment websites. Exhibit 3H on p.126 shows MACPA's history of ROA from 1998 to 2012 (founded 1901), in terms of its components ROS and

ATO. In such a graph the most favorable position is toward upper right corner where both ROS and ATO are increasing incrementally.

ROA is a measure of management's effectiveness in producing profits from all the available assets. It was developed by Alfred Sloan in collaboration with Donaldson Brown at General Motors in the 1920s. This rigorous version of return on investment helped Sloan exceed internal business performance targets year after year, until his goal was reached, which was to create a larger automobile company than Henry Ford. For decades, ROA was kept a competitive secret until one of Sloan's finance team took charge as the Treasurer at Du Pont, where he began using ROA to drive DuPont's business to higher levels of performance. Eventually, ROA was revealed publicly at a meeting of the American Management Association in 1952, where Lou Mobley was in attendance. Now, ROA is widely used as a measure of management effectiveness.

Sloan and Brown discovered deeper insights about ROA through a mathematical breakdown of the basic formula into its component parts.

Return on Asset = Net Income/Average Total Assets

or alternatively . . .

Return on Asset = Return on Sales times Asset Turnover

where . . .

Return on Sales (ROS) = Net Profit/Sales Revenue
Asset Turnover (ATO) = Sales Revenue/Average Total Assets

Notice that the second ROA formula mentioned above equals the first formula because when ROS (Net/Sales) is multiplied by ATO (Sales/Assets), mathematically Sales in numerator and denominator cancel each other leaving Net Income divided by Average Total Assets.

Mobley's (mob-lee) alternative math approach offers guidance about how to steward ROA improvement. More specifically, there is a need to focus on improving ROS %, which indicates how much of every dollar of sales revenue makes it to profit. There is a need to increase ATO, which can be accomplished by more productive use of assets to generate sales and by selling unproductive assets. The math shows there is a cost in terms of lower ROA that comes from sitting on unproductive assets.

Although Sloan pioneered this mathematical breakdown of ROA, this competitive secret was revealed by DuPont, and consequently it became known as the DuPont formula.

Historically, managers normally find that improving ROS comes easier than engineering improved ATO. At IBM, Mobley found that it was best to have relatively equal incremental improvements in both efficiency (ROS) and effectiveness (ATO). These should be monitored selectively and steadily instead of focusing on one over the other. This insight guided Mobley executive leadership students in making realistic pro forma projections.

Notice Exhibit 3C on p.121, Balance Sheet for ZYY. This is the snapshot at the close of business on the last day of the year. Balance Sheets possess an eternal equation where Assets are equal to the sum of Liabilities and Owner's Equity (A = L + E). All Assets come from either borrowed funds (liabilities) or from stockholders' contributions (initial stock purchases and undistributed profits).

Let us assume the total assets at the end of the previous year were equal to the total assets at the end of 2015.

To calculate ROA for ZYY = Net Income/Average Total Assets
= \$122,950/\$1,111,800
= 11.1%

Comparison to historic data and industry percentages would provide insights. For many industries, ROA generally ranges from 5 to 15 percent. There is more on this measure in Chapter 4.

Ways to drive ROA higher:
- Attract customers even if selling prices are raised, which will drive revenues higher.
- Manage supply chain relationships and contracts to minimize costs.
- Manage operating costs through creating internal efficiencies and eliminating waste.

- Intelligently direct spending for marketing and advertising to drive revenues.
- Skillfully select new staff and create incentives for effective execution of business plans.
- Determine how to reduce investments in fixed assets through more effective business processes. Lower total assets utilized will boost ROA.

The Financial Scoreboard: Reconciling the Three Bottom Lines

Exhibit 3F on p.124 shows the Financial Scoreboard (FSB) spreadsheet as originally developed by Chuck Kremer at the request of Jahn Ballard. A powerful tool for forecasting financial results and for informing non-financial staff, FSB shows the interconnectedness of the three financial statements (balance sheet, income statement, and cash flow statement). A demo of this spreadsheet, can be acquired from www.MOSupgrade.com/MLA/Library.

Notice the following features of the FSB:
- The spreadsheet shows how the year-end balance sheet is derived from three financial statement data sources: beginning of year balance sheet, the income statement transaction summaries, and the cash flow summaries.
- All three bottom lines are shown in the bottom right corner table.
- Cash Flow Statement data are shown according to the Direct Method and thereby revealing a clear, simple understanding of how cash is accumulated and spent.

The FSB tools are especially helpful for a Decision Team that wants to maintain a clear vision of what is happening.

Exhibit 3G on p.125 "Financial Scoreboard Accounts Mapping Template" shows how to map enterprise financial accounts with FSB universal format accounts. Required combining of account balances must be mapped to the FSB template before entering data. Use of the scoreboard assists with the Reality Check by developing a financial "big picture" baseline for the enterprise. After the actual historic data has been entered, it becomes straightforward to input budget data for the next period. The demo offers a one-period scoreboard to analyze an Income Statement and two Balance Sheets.

Jeff Lueken, CEO, Lueken's Food Stores, Reflects on the Value of Financial Literacy

There are plenty of resources to teach one the "what" of financial literacy, but none that I found besides BARD that can teach executives and managers, as well as line and supervisory staff, the "hows" and the "whys". It is abundantly clear to me that we have to have our people meaningfully involved. There has to be a clear and obvious picture of the finances and the "value propositions." We have to teach people how to leverage their and our information as leaders going forward while engaging everyone in improving our business results. Otherwise, we strand the capital of our people's direct job experience that we invest paycheck after paycheck to create.

If leaders decide they don't need to teach people about finances, and they don't need to fully engage people in their business' value creation activity, then they are throwing away operating cash and other current common threads that make for success.

In the next chapter, we will define how the 10 key drivers of business performance generate the three bottom lines, and how to identify candidate system-level key performance indicator candidates to monitor and direct activities more effectively and precisely.

References

Kremer, C., Rizzuto, R., and Case, J. (2000). *Managing by the Numbers: A Commonsense Guide to Understanding and Using Your Company's Financials.* Cambridge, MA: Inc/Perseus

Kremer, C. (2002). *The Use and Abuse of Financial Statements.* Maryland Association of CPAs Ezine.

CHAPTER 4

Link Financial Drivers, Disconnects, and KPIs

Ballard's Alignment and Reporting Disciplines

1. *Map and Identify*: Map the sequence of VCAs; identify disconnects.
2. *Analyze and Project*: Three-bottom-line analysis with rolling cash flow projections.
3. *Define and Link*: Define financial drivers and disconnects; develop key KPIs linking activities and transactions.
4. *Engage and Align*: Engage leaders and staff by aligning on both true core facts and desired outcomes.
5. *Monitor and Report*: Regularly monitor performance in periodic huddles using outcome-driven agendas.

Ballard's Dictum: Activity Precedes Transaction in All Cases

In this chapter, you will see how to begin creating behavioral and financial scoreboards to effectively guide the enterprise toward greater value creation excellence. We begin by defining the characteristics of Key Performance Indicators (KPIs). You will get guidance from Maryland Association of Certified Public Accountants (MACPA)'s experience of answering this key question: Which crucial few of the many, many things that could be measured, should be measured, in order to achieve enterprise objectives?

Next, you will learn about the 10 internal financial drivers that combine mathematically to produce Three-Bottom-Line Results, and how strong KPIs may directly affect one or more of those drivers. In addition, you will discover two external financial drivers that are important for bankers and investors in their assessment of enterprise health. Along the way will be opportunities to appreciate how nonfinancial, activity-related factors affect progressive improvement in financial measure results.

Finally, we show how MACPA's development of a Material Assumptions Index helped validate the accuracy of their pro forma financial statements, while building unanimity on the core facts of the enterprise.

Key Performance Indicators

Beyond monitoring the overall health of the organization, senior leadership needs to determine imperatives for improving operational capabilities. Focus on a few targeted high-priority issues can produce handsome benefits.

KPIs have been part of the management scheme of organizations for decades. No one set of KPIs fits all organizations. Ideally, these measures come from a meaningful dialog with both customers and stakeholders about how they view the value-creating processes of the enterprise. For example, many business-to-business enterprises have discovered that their leanly managed customers desire shorter lead times (i.e., number of days from order to delivery of goods or services) and on-time delivery of products. In some case, a critical KPI is percentage of orders delivered (or shipped) on-time. This measure tells everyone how effectively the enterprise is committed to achieving this important aspect of customer relations.

A rigorous KPI links both an operating activities component with a financial data point (or resource-impact component) that together link to an internal or external customer.

A well-designed set of KPIs can become a crucial focus for an enterprise to thrive, both at the whole system level, and within each of the numbered value-creating activity accounts on the Chart of Activities. KPIs are a measure for focusing on overall workflow, and how that activity flow relates to both customer results (external and internal), as well as overall financial results. A rigorous and validated KPI will include:

1. A measure of behavior—data showing the result(s) of activity
2. A measure of the financial impact—the economic results

A KPI uses the metaphor of a mathematical ratio, one that links a behavioral data measurement point with a related financial outcome number, and then both are linked with an internal or external customer served. Ballard Method KPIs can be linked at the whole system level directly to operating cash flow, profit, or return outcomes (at least one of the three bottom lines) through one or more key internal financial drivers.

A KPI looks like this: **Behavioral data/Financial data**

Behavioral data—The workplace numbers we use to measure activities undertaken within the Value Cycle to create value by getting each job done excellently for customers.

Financial data—The accounting side—the money. What it costs us to make products and deliver services. How much we charge customers for the products and services we deliver. How much profit is left after all that? What financial data point is most related to these activities?

If the same KPI measures the impacts of more than one constraint in the Value-Creating Activity accounts, it will have more leverage to improve results, and tend to be a good candidate for getting at the primary constraint. Once validated and worked with over time, a KPI may become a master measure, that is, part of Standard Operating Procedure as a now-proven Key Leading Indicator for future financial results. A KPI may also be retired, or become secondary to a newly emerged master measure. KPIs can also be linked to each other in a hierarchy that is based on the whole work system's mandates and performance priorities.

Unfortunately, most KPIs in today's corporate management approach do not fulfill the above criteria, and in some cases are actually sources of fragmentation, instead of integration.

Here are examples of two master measure KPIs that emerged from an all-hands staff engagement at MACPA, and two more general examples. Refer to Chapter 2, Exhibit 2E on p.119 to see how these items connect to the MACPA Value Cycle Map.

#1 KPI Sample: Seminar Revenue Shortfall (related to VCA #5 in the MACPA Value Cycle)

- **Disconnect**: Need better measures on effectiveness of teams promoting seminars
- **Math:** Seminar Revenue Shortfall/Seminar Revenue Budget Goal

- **Linkage to Key Internal Financial Driver**: COS (Cost of Sales)/Total Revenues
- **Why it mattered**: Seminars were MACPA's second highest revenue source after professional dues.

#2 KPI Sample: *Market Enrollment (related to VCA #1 in the MACPA Value Cycle)*

- **Disconnect**: Flat membership growth
- **Math**: Total Number of CPAs Enrolled/Total Number of Eligible CPAs in State
- **Linkage to Key Internal Financial Driver**: MSGA/Total Revenues
- **Why it mattered**: MACPA has been holding steady at around two-thirds of CPAs in Maryland being members compared to other State CPA Societies, which have had shrinking potential market penetration. However, MACPA wanted to drive improvement in market penetration after stalling and holding at 66% for many years.

#3 KPI Sample: *Profit Capacity Utilization (broad measure)*

- **Need**: Track profitability over the square footage of office space utilized
- **Math**: Total Square Footage/Profit per Employee
- **Linkage to Key Internal Financial Driver**: MSGA/Sales or Salaries/Sales Revenue
- **Why** it **mattered**: Relates profitability to return on physical plant

#4 KPI Sample: *Total Revenues per Employee (broad measure)*

- **Need**: Track relationship of headcount to revenues
- **Math**: Total Revenues/Number of Employees
- **Linkage to Key Internal Financial Driver**: MSGA/Sales or Salaries/Sales Revenue

- **Why it mattered**: To keep control over tendency to hire more people without anticipating the financial impact.

Because every Management Operating System is unique, all KPIs do not necessarily apply as useful tools in different work cultures even in the same industry. When tacit knowledge revealed produces a unanimously affirmed master KPI metric, it is often surprisingly simple and common sense. The KPI just needed to emerge through the right sequence of questions that find out their activities driving the key transactions.

Some KPIs will become Standard Operating Procedure, others will provide a temporary focus that ceases to be needed after the underlying constraint is resolved. The key is to have a method to continually and accurately assess which KPIs continue to bring value and insight.

Brainstorm Nontransaction Measures

For at least a dozen important disconnects, define a nonfinancial measure of activity results that would indicate whether an improvement initiative was working. Define the financial compliment the activities impact. Then pick the three to five most likely to be the primary constraint to value throughput for exploration as a master measure. If it is not perfectly clear to you what is being suggested, read on until it is clear, then brainstorm a dozen candidates, and pick the five most likely suspects for the primary constraint.

Staying Focused on Business Process Improvements

Which crucial few of the many, many things that could be measured, should be measured, in order to achieve our purposes?

When the time comes, the senior team chooses its three to five most value-eroding disconnects/breakdowns, then tests and measures to validate their accuracy and usefulness. Depending on which disconnects and candidate KPIs are chosen, the senior team may need to carefully (using the same method) engage certain key staff to help further consider, identify, and test the assumptions underlying the choice of that measure.

Let us refresh what we mean by a "disconnect," which creates waste in the value stream. A disconnect (or breakdown) creates non-value-added activities such as bottlenecks, waiting times, excessive movement of resources or people, duplicated efforts, and other constraints. A disconnect is anything making our individual jobs more difficult, or that stops or makes the Value Cycle flow less smoothly. Here are some additional points about disconnects.

- A cluster of one or more decisions and actions that generate unintended (usually*) outcomes, which limit value throughput in the enterprise
- Inefficiencies and ineffectiveness within the enterprise's sequence of value-creating activities, usually existing in the hand-offs between upstream or downstream value-creating activities
- A validated disconnect is one that is first unanimously affirmed by all staff concerned, and is also then linked directly to at least one Value-Creating Activity and can usually be linked to at least one KPI.
- * There can be both intended and unintended outcomes from disconnects that are created or perpetuated, because of unhealthy internal competition driven by incentivizing one person or group to do things that they think will make them look good, or make a perceived internal rival look bad.

In developing a useful KPI, it is critical to understand how disconnects in a specific activity affect the drivers of the broader business system. A system-level KPI will directly connect to one or more of following 10 internal Key Financial Drivers.

Ten Key Internal Financial Drivers

Which few of these drivers are most crucial to your enterprise's value delivery?

The 10 Key Financial Drivers provide feedback, or a scoreboard, that is relevant for any economic enterprise.

The 10 Internal Key Financial Drivers of All Three-Bottom-Line Outcomes

These 10 internal financial drivers mathematically create the three bottom lines presented in Chapter 3. First, let us examine an overview of the 10, and then break them down for further insights.

Overview of the 10 Internal Drivers:

1 Cash Driver = Operating Cash Flow/Sales Revenue

1 Efficiency Driver = Net Profit/Sales Revenue, often called Return on Sales (ROS)

1 Effectiveness Driver = Sales Revenue/Average Assets, often called Capital or Asset Turnover (ATO)

3 Expense Drivers (which four below can be mixed and matched to meet reporting needs)
  ○ Cost of Sales or Goods Sold/Sales Revenue
  ○ MSGA (i.e., Marketing, Selling, General and Admin Expenses)/Sales Revenue
  ○ Salaries Expense/Sales Revenue in service and distribution companies
  ○ R&D (Research and Development Expenses)/Sales Revenue if driving product or service innovation

3 Turnover Metrics: Receivables, Payables, and Inventory Days (details below)

1 Fixed Asset Driver = 5 Net Profit/Average Net Fixed Assets

Now, let us dissect each of the 10 internal financial drivers to understand how management gains insights for optimizing operating results.

We conclude with the cash conversion cycle that ties it all together to build reserves intentionally.

Key Financial Driver #1: Cash Driver = Operating Cash Flow/ Sales Revenue

BARD's Enterprise Fuel Gauge

To calculate this measure, find the Operating Cash Flow as the first subtotal on the Cash Flow Statement. Then divide this number by Sales

Revenue shown on the Income Statement. This metric answers the question, "How many dollars of Operating Cash Flow go in or out (if negative) of the bank account for every dollar of Sales?"

This metric is similar to ROS. However, instead of using Net Income in the numerator, we substitute Operating Cash Flow. We can think of it as a cash basis version of ROS. For a healthy enterprise, this metric is positive and growing. We like to see average growth of 10 percent or more year over year. But, this level of growth may not happen consistently because of external and internal factors, which could include lack of agreement internally about what needs to be improved. There may also be fluctuations due to variations in the economy or industry cycle in addition to enterprise-level conditions.

Very few senior leaders even calculate this number. It is the single most powerful financial results driver in the Ballard's Alignment and Reporting Disciplines (BARD) key driver toolbox. If leaders and their staff develop a common understanding of how this driver connects to what they all do every day, almost everything else just starts falling into line. For a CEO or senior leader, this metric provides an excellent view for gauging progress toward operating activities excellence that shows ten dollars and ten cents of OCF being deposited for every $100 of sales.

For ZYY Corporation the Cash Driver is determined by this formula:

Cash Driver = \$124,300/\$1,225,000 = 10.1%

This compares to approximately the ROS percentage that is based on accrual approach to earnings instead of cash-generated value. The Cash Driver may be nearly equal to ROS, or higher, or lower than ROS. Companies with high investments in depreciable assets often show higher Cash Driver metrics compared to their ROS.

Key Financial Driver #2: Return on Sales = Net Income/Net Sales Revenue

ROS is a measure of management's *efficiency* in running the enterprise. This ratio of two key numbers from the Income Statement indicates what percentage of every dollar of revenues is realized as profit. It answers the question, "How many dollars of Profit did we generate for every dollar of Sales Revenue?"

Each industry will have its own distinct average for ROS, with a distribution of industry members around its average. For example, in the retail grocery business the ROS is usually 1 to 3 percent. On the other hand, equipment-leasing companies may have ROS in the 30 to 40 percent range. Many businesses operate with ROS in the range of 5 to 12 percent. Each year, the goal is to try to drive toward a higher ROS.

ROS is a key metric for assessing the overall efficiency of managing the day-to-day activities of an enterprise. How well are you managing the attraction of sales transactions? How well are you choosing or updating the pricing of products/services? How well are you managing the expenses that support sales-generating activities? If the ROS is 5 percent, it means that $.05 of every dollar of sales makes it to the bottom line of Net Profit.

Notice that the ROS for ZYY Corporation (Exhibit 3B on p.120— Income Statement) was 10 percent for the year. That means, 10 percent of every dollar of sales revenue survived as profit, based on accrual accounting methods. With industry data and prior years' data, it would be possible to evaluate the current situation of ROS.

Key Financial Driver #3: Asset Turnover = Sales Revenue /Average Assets

Asset Turnover (ATO) is a measure of leadership ***effectiveness*** in running a sustainable enterprise. The Effectiveness Driver is calculated by dividing Sales by Average Total Assets. It answers the question, "How many dollars of Sales did we generate for every dollar of Assets employed?"

The goal is to improve this relationship slightly every period. For ZYY Corporation, the metric is calculated as follows:

ATO Effectiveness Driver = $1,225,000/$1,111,800 = 11.1%.
It would support effective evaluation of internal performance to compare this result with industry data.

Key Financial Driver #4: Cost of Sales (COS) or Goods Sold % = COGS/Sales Revenue

COGS/Sales will be appropriate for merchandising (either wholesale or retail) or manufacturing enterprises. It shows what percentage of the revenues is consumed by the cost of purchases or manufacturing of products. COS will tend to be used similarly in service enterprises.

Sales Revenue minus Cost of Goods Sold is called Gross Profit (GP). For ZYY Corporation in Chapter 3—Exhibit 3B Income Statement, we find that the company's CGS% = 43.3%. Notice the inverse of this percentage (56.7 percent) is GP. These two percentages are always mirror opposites. In Driver #2, we use the data in the column to the right of the dollar amounts, that is, we use the percentage relationships with respect to Sales Revenue.

This metric is not influenced by any of the Operating Expense categories such as marketing, sales, administrative, or general expenses. **In COS or COGS%, the focus is on monitoring costs of acquiring and creating inventory in relation to the revenues generated by selling inventory.** Of course, the idea is to drive COGS% lower and thereby drive GP% higher.

Factors that will drive COS or COGS% lower
- Lower prices from suppliers
- Choosing higher markups over cost to determine sales prices
- Leaner, more efficient manufacturing methods resulting in lower costs per unit

A blind passion to lower COS or COGS% and thereby increase GP% could have unintended impacts. Managers need to anticipate the dangers of driving down costs without considering the consequences of poor choices.

Possible downsides of lowering COS or COGS%
- Lower prices from suppliers might mean lower quality.
- Higher markups might cause customers to look for substitutes.
- Lower costs of manufacturing might be caused by cutting corners and lower quality.

Key Financial Driver #5: Operating Expense % = Total Operating Expenses or MSGA/Sales Revenue

In this metric, we examine the relationship of all operating expenses to sales revenue. Operating expenses can be broken down according to four types: Marketing, Selling, General and Administrative (MSGA). In the early years of operations, an enterprise may experience stepping up expenditures to build basic support capacities in the operating expense subcategories. **As an enterprise grows in scale, this percentage will often tend to decline because the incremental costs of supporting operations tend to decline as sales revenues increase.** Depending on measurement requirements, it could also be helpful to further break down MSGA into presenting each of its four component parts.

For ZYY Corporation, the Operating Expenses are 44.2 percent of Sales Revenue.

Key Financial Driver #6: Human Resources % = Salaries Expense/Sales Revenue

This percentage is especially appropriate for service or distribution enterprises and manufacturing enterprises that are not R&D intensive. It describes how much of Sales revenues are consumed by Salaries Expense. The better a company gets at leveraging the talents of its employees, the lower this percentage becomes. Lower is better.

Or alternatively for asset intensive and R&D manufacturing, use this driver:

R&D% = Research and Development Expenses/Sales Revenue

The R&D% shows how much of Revenues are consumed by R&D expenses. As a company matures, it is normal to expect a decline in these percentages. As the tacit knowledge within an organization becomes shared and more transparent, employees become more effective and R&D often gets better managed to produce new products.

These two metrics are control points for leveraging the tacit knowledge of employees to produce revenues. As the organization becomes more effective in value creation, anticipate how these percentages should change. Salaries% should decline. R&D% should decline unless cash reserve surpluses allow greater innovation risks.

The breakdowns on both salaries and R&D expenses reside within Operating Expenses and are not shown separately in the example of ZYY Corporation data from Chapter 3.

Factors that drive Salaries% lower:

- Elimination of waste and unproductive capacity
- Improved selection of qualified personnel that boosts productivity
- Implementation of training and technology to boost productivity

Factors that drive R&D% lower:

- Improved selection of R&D projects resulting in higher number of projects made operational.
- Improved ability to execute business plans results in higher profitability.
- Scaling of R&D efforts allows reuse of R&D productive capacities.

Next we consider the Turnover Drivers (#'s 7 to 9) to monitor the efficiencies of collections for receivables, payments of debts to suppliers, and the time needed to sell inventory on hand. Improvement across these metrics enhances the sales cycle, that is, the time between purchasing inventory and collecting cash from customers. Managers seek to increase all three metrics by various tactics. Each of the key driver measures is created by capturing a piece of data from an Income Statement account, and dividing it by another piece of data from a Balance Sheet or Cash account. Look for the discussion of Cash Conversion Cycle at the end of this chapter.

Key Financial Driver #7: Accounts Receivable Turnover = Net Credit Sales Revenues/Average Accts Receivable

Account Receivable Turnover indicates how many times in a year the average of accounts receivable is collected from customers. For ZYY Corporation statements shown as exhibits in Chapter 3, we will assume that all sales made for the year were credit sales and the amount of accounts receivable at year-end represents an average level of receivables.

For ZYY Corporation, AR Turnover = $1,225,000/$95,000
= 12.9 times

To determine the average number of days to collect receivables, divide AR Turnover into 365 days.

Average number of days to collect receivables
= 365 days/12.9 times = 28.3 days

If ZYY Corporation offers normal payment terms of 30 days, then the average collection is slightly lower than the payment expectation. Normally, a CFO would like to see this measure as in this example—below the 30-day term.

This is the first key number for the cash collection cycle. The goal of leadership is to minimize this number.

Ways to decrease number of days to collect receivables:
- More strict credit granting policies for new customers
- More attractive incentives for early payment, for example, discounts
- Better communications with late-paying customers to facilitate collections

Key Financial Driver #8: Accounts Payable
Turnover = Purchases from Suppliers/Average Accts Payable

The AP Turnover indicates the number of times per year that average accounts payable are paid for credit-based purchases of inventory. Leadership's goal is to extend this time period as much as possible, to allow use of cash for other purposes. To calculate this percentage for ZYY Corporation, we will assume that the amount of credit purchases of inventory during the year is $500,000.

For ZYY Corporation, AP Turnover = $500,000/$53,000 = 9.43 times

To determine the average number of days to disburse funds to settle accounts payable, divide AP Turnover into 365 days.

Average number of days to settle payables
= 365 days/9.43 times = 38.7 days

In an enterprise that wants to extend the time needed to pay for supplier invoices, a CFO wants to see a higher number of days because it allows more flexibility in the use of cash resources.

Ways to increase the number of days to settle payables owed:

- Negotiate longer terms for payment, for example, 60 days instead of 30 days.
- Negotiate lower penalties for late payments.

Key Financial Driver #9: Inventory Turnover = Cost of Goods Sold/Average Inventory

Inventory Turnover indicates the number of times per year that the average level of inventory is sold. Higher inventory turnover is desirable. Simply take the Cost of Goods Sold from the Income Statement and divide by the Average Inventory level.

For the ZYY Corporation case study, we will assume that the ending inventory shown on the Balance Sheet ($62,000) represents a normal level of inventory.

For ZYY Corporation, Inventory Turnover = $530,000/$62,000 = 8.54 times

To determine the average number of days to sell inventory, divide Inventory Turnover into 365 days.

**Average number of days to sell inventory
= 365 days/8.54 times = 42.7 days**

An enterprise wants to reduce the time needed to sell inventory. CFOs want to drive this key measure lower.

Ways to reduce the number of days to sell average available inventory:

- Improve sales capacity for selling products.
- Improve channels of distribution.
- Develop lean supply chain relationships to shorten lead times for inventory replacement. This leads to lower levels of inventory on-hand, boosts Inventory Turnover and reduces the average number of days to sell inventory.

Key Financial Driver #10: Fixed Asset Driver = Net Income/ Average Net Fixed Assets

The Fixed Asset Driver is calculated by taking the bottom-line Net Income from the Income Statement and dividing by the Average Net Fixed Assets from the Balance Sheet. This measures the effectiveness of leadership regarding Fixed Assets. It is a form of return on internal investment that provides a feedback loop about how much profitability was generated during the year as a percentage of the average level of fixed assets utilized.

For ZYY Corporation the metric is calculated based on the assumption that year-end fixed assets were approximately equal to beginning-of-year fixed assets.

$$\textbf{Fixed Asset Driver} = \$122,950/\$800,000 = 15.4\%$$

Cash Conversion Cycle

Within the 10 Internal Key Financial Drivers, the enterprise's cash conversion cycle can be an important means for monitoring and controlling the velocity of cash flow from operations. The cash conversion cycle indicates the average number of days needed to convert inventories into cash inflows. Business teams that are able to minimize the cash conversion cycle will tend to minimize the need to tap lines of credit.

We showed in this chapter how to calculate the three components of the cash conversion cycle where each of the elements was described as an ancillary concept to Key Financial Drivers 7 to 9. Notice the calculation of the days to collect or pay related to each of those core drivers.

In the example of ZYY Corporation, the Cash Conversion Cycle is calculated as:

Add:
Average # of days to sell inventory = 365 days/8.54 times = 42.7 days
Average # of days to collect receivables = 365 days/11.84 times = 28.3 days

Deduct:
Average # of days to settle payables = 365 days/9.43 times = (38.7 days)
Cash Conversion Cycle   **32.3 days**

The goal is to minimize the number of days to convert cash back to cash. The cash conversion cycle is positively affected by these business objectives:

- Sell inventory faster or reduce amount of inventory on hand.
- Watch carefully credit-granting policies and customer follow-up procedures to avoid slow or no-pay customers.
- Seek longer payment terms without penalties from vendors.

Two External Key Financial Drivers

In addition to the 10 internal key financial drivers, there are two external financial drivers that keep management focused on the two external stakeholders to whom one reports:

Banker's Driver—Total Debt/Total Assets.

This percentage describes how much of Total Assets were generated by taking on debt. If this relationship gets too debt heavy, banks will stop lending. Responsible leaders know this and want to develop their Balance Sheets so they will continue to be attractive to lenders, to minimize interest costs, and to assure an adequate source of funds when needed. Banks like to see the percentage less than 60 percent and will stop lending at 65 percent.

Investor's Driver—Net Profit/Average Stockholder's Equity, also known as Return on Equity (ROE)

This percentage is another form of return on investment. It describes how much profit was earned with respect to the sum of two investments made by stockholders, that is, the initial funds given to the company years ago when the first stock issue was sold to investors, AND also the amount of undistributed profits since the beginning of the business. So, the denominator represents the amount of money from investors with which management could work to build the enterprise. Potential investors typically look at both ROA and ROE as indicators of management effectiveness. These percentages are mathematically equivalent when there is no debt.

Now, let us see how the assembly of both historical data (actuals) and financial projections for the next operating period serve to get people focused on urgency to plan and act to correct risk(s) of being outside specified requirements in the upcoming financial picture.

MACPA Internal Key Drivers Scoreboard Supports Accurate Pro Formas

Which value-creating activities impact which Key Drivers crucial to success in your enterprise?

Exhibit 4A on p.127 shows MACPA's Scoreboard of Internal Key Financial Drivers using actual data from 2009 to 2011 and forecasted data for 2012. Notice that these initial projections predict negative profitability for 2012. This report was generated by the forecasting capabilities of the Financial Scoreboard software tools—a free one-period demo and orientation template is available on the book's website—www.MOSupgrade.com/MLA /Library. For managers who want to create what-if scenarios, the Financial Scoreboard is the perfect instrument to put together financial projections without needing the assistance of an accountant.

When the Senior Team works together to develop projections for coming year(s), they collaborate on detailing an index of Material Assumptions like Exhibit 4B on p.128 for MACPA. On one page in plain English the anticipated and/or engineered business changes are expressed. The agreement on these assumptions paves the way for a common view of the future and related changes in operations. This collaboration opens the door for senior leaders to engage the next level of associates that takes the form of "how do we accomplish this together." A Material Assumptions Index should be focused to give both financial and nonfinancial staff critical understanding of the key financial drivers that their daily activities impact, as well as to align internal and external finance professionals.

In 2011, CEO Tom Hood and CFO Skip Falatco were looking at an unprofitable projection for 2012 based on MACPA's Material Assumptions. Through inquiry into the numbers, Hood and Falatco could see there had been a positive windfall in Other Income during 2011 that actually boosted that year's profitability as an isolated event. This windfall had not been adjusted out as one of the Material Assumptions. Hood and Falatco were able to take corrective actions to lead the organization back toward a profitable picture by 2013 by focusing on assuring positive operating cash flow in 2012. This example illustrates the power of combining operational and financial tools to enhance leadership capabilities.

By combining material assumptions with the Financial Scoreboard view of financial statements, Hood and Falatco also accomplished another profound result. They had a financial picture to share with nonfinancial staff that included projections (Pro Formas) that would be accepted by any banker as a basis for performing on loan covenants. In fact, many bankers would not have Pro Formas where the financial statements are both reconciled with each other, and with all 12 key drivers. This capacity to more than satisfy banking covenant specifications was a crucial financial tool for Tom Hood when he was a CFO in private industry, before assuming the mantle of stewardship for the MACPA.

Hood shares how he and the CFO applied these banker-level Pro Formas with MACPA staff.

> After we oriented the whole team to Three-Bottom-Line performance and showed them how to project results in the future, we looked at the story of our last 13 years since 1999, so everyone could see how our history is reflected in our total revenue, profit and operating cash flow record. We then showed them the loss scenario that was likely to happen if we did not change that outcome together. We developed a report that showed financial details that were relevant to key functions each person and team performs, and then we had them sort into work teams to explore the data and look creatively at how to really pop their results for the next 4 months. We called it our 'Hit the Gas' Huddle. — Tom Hood, CEO, MACPA

This completes the theory and applied illustrations about the 10 internal drivers and 2 external drivers that support managing all three bottom lines. The 10 internal financial drivers provide a continuous feedback scoreboard that is relevant for any economic enterprise when connected to Material Assumptions and validated KPIs.

Remember, the whole enterprise system can only function as well as its worst constraint(s), what Jack Stack (author of *The Great Game of Business*), calls the key vulnerabilities, or what is sometimes called the weakest link in the chain. Those constraints can be found through a systematic process of discovery—applying the scientific method to test and validate any assumptions about what are the greatest constraints, or what could be called system disconnects. The question is how to find those few dynamic constraints, vulnerabilities, or disconnects, such that when they are improved, the whole system's value throughput will automatically be improved across the board.

Legend has it that back when Agilent was still part of HP Labs, a group invented a rolling device that would meet a heart attack victim at the door of a hospital emergency room (ER), as they were coming off the ambulance. A spring-loaded wrist cuff and a couple of skin sensors were put on the heart attack patient, at which time they would immediately have 30 data points on their physiological state.

In the ER's where this device was piloted, they doubled the savings of lives by having all that relevant physical data immediately upon arrival. Several of the teams over the first year noticed independently that four numbers were coming up more often in the post-mortem debriefs for each case. In multiple test hospitals they decided independently to make a new protocol, in which they only checked those four numbers, instead of all 30 of them. When they implemented that, they doubled the savings of lives again!

What they found was that by checking those four numbers, they could get to all 30 data points in two steps, because the other 26 all connected to one of the four. In the same way, in any organization, there are only a small group of very specific behavioral disconnects that govern, or constrain, overall performance. The million-dollar questions are what are those key disconnects, and what master measures will support the highest returns, that are not cancelled out by too high a cost for the measurement to be implemented?

Chapter Summary and Conclusions

In this chapter, we learned about three sets of performance measurement tools:

- A KPI method geared toward tracking and improving value creation by linking measurements of value-creating activities to related financial transactions and/or summaries.
- The 10 Internal Financial Drivers serve as a few valuable feedback loops to the leadership team about the overall health of the enterprise. We provided a sample of the Financial Scoreboard that reveals Three Bottom Lines, 12 Key Drivers, and two formats of Cash Statements.

- And, finally, we observed how MACPA's senior team created Material Assumptions for each account on the Pro Forma financial statements to document reasoning and supporting data, as well as to most accurately track progress on improving specific activities and financial outcomes.

For the Facilitator or Senior System Steward (CEO or designate), the next chapter shows how to use the Reality Check documents. These draft documents serve as the basis for facilitating engagement of Senior Leaders in the learning adventure to transform enterprise to higher levels of operational achievement and employee satisfaction. It is a privilege to share these critical methods to successfully pull leaders, and then eventually, staff, into a widening circle of transparent inquiry and unanimity about how value is either created, or destroyed by disconnects and breakdowns.

Jeff Lueken, CEO, Lueken's Food Stores Reflects on Value of the CEO Reality Check

The Reality Check allowed me a clearer view of the landscape ahead. What is truly needed with a completeness that feels like it is the whole puzzle. It has simplified the core set of information required to make better decisions and amplified the key areas of the business that need immediate attention.

I think a CEO of any business, would benefit from taking themselves through a their own personal CEO Reality Check on how enterprise value creation links to transactions. The clarity it offers both in terms of who and what the business truly is (its "value" proposition), and its financials, makes obvious sense. Just the financial aspect itself has great worth, even though it is in fact not the key element of a Reality Check. The picture we, as a senior team, now have of our landscape going forward from the Reality Check is the de facto benchmark for evaluating all of our strategies and tactics moving forward.

In Chapter 5, you will discover the wisdom of pulling Senior Team members into the BARD dialogue instead of pushing it upon them. We discovered these adept alignment techniques through years of experimentation in over 50 community and commercial enterprises.

CHAPTER 5

Engage and Align Senior Leadership

Ballard's Alignment and Reporting Disciplines (BARD)

1. *Map and Identify*: Map the sequence of VCAs; identify disconnects.
2. *Analyze and Project*: Three-bottom-line analysis with rolling cash flow projections.
3. *Define and Link*: Define financial drivers and disconnects; develop key KPIs linking activities and transactions.
4. *Engage and Align*: Engage leaders and staff by aligning on both true core facts and desired outcomes.
5. *Monitor and Report*: Regularly monitor performance in periodic huddles using outcome-driven agendas.

In this chapter, you as CEO, Senior System Steward, or facilitator will see how to apply what you have learned in the CEO Reality Check through your personal engagement in the first three Ballard disciplines. When a senior leader personally does the work, he or she models the way for others to follow with credibility. With this authentic experience in hand, the leader (often the CEO) is prepared to engage others in the senior team. But, the question is how to engage them so they will be receptive to BARD? In this chapter, you dear reader, can benefit from our focus and experience engaging and aligning senior management, and then their broader circles of colleagues.

This journey of transformation will not occur overnight. It will likely take months or longer to really take hold, and several years to mature enough to be self-perpetuating. After associates see that senior leaders are serious about initiating constructive dialogue for improving the business by listening effectively and reporting transparently, they will respond with equal enthusiasm when they can see there is a real audience that wants to hear and act on their years of experience with business processes. This dialogue can serve to usher in a more mature measurement culture, resulting in increased job satisfaction, improved morale, and higher performance.

So far, through the processes described in Chapters 2 to 4, we have followed a logical path of inquiry that entailed developing these documents:

- Chart of (value-creating) Activities first draft (Chapter 2)
- List of all disconnects/breakdowns in the value-creating activities (VCAs) sequence (Chapter 2)
- List of three to five prioritized key performance indicators (KPIs) of activity results for correcting key disconnects in crucial VCAs (Chapter 4)
- Conducting Three-Bottom-Line Performance analysis described and then demonstrated by an Maryland Association of Certified Public Accountants (MACPA) Financial Scoreboard and Material Assumptions (Chapter 3)
- KPIs linking VCAs and Disconnects to one or more of 10 Key Financial drivers (Chapter 4)

All personal work products, at each step of the tacit knowledge mining process, should be kept private. It is very important that previous work products are not shared until the next invited persons have in writing, shared their viewpoints on value creation and destruction, so the senior team, and then others, can then see their personal insights included with those of the CEO and CFO as their starting point to engagement.

In this chapter you will learn how to engage people in the adventure of BARD in ways that lead to excellence in enterprise performance. Employee engagement requires a positive and receptive tone at the top, and a willingness to involve staff as leaders in the enterprise. Are you ready for a practical exercise in committed leadership and clear communication?

Tone at the Top

According to Kirsten Davidson, Head of Employer Brand at Glassdoor, a recent study by their Chief Economist, Andrew Chamberlain, shows that salary has a statistically small effect on job satisfaction. Instead, the study reveals that "the most important factors influencing job satisfaction are culture and values, career-advancement opportunities and the opinion of senior leadership" (Davidson, 2016).

Glassdoor Inc. collaborates with Human Capital Media Advisory Group, the research arm of Workforce Magazine, in developing its annual list of 100 Best Places to Work. For 2016, the Top five consisted of American Express, Google, Accenture, USAA, and AT&T. People love working at these companies. Beyond publicly available HR performance data, employees provide feedback about why they enjoy working at these places. There are seven common traits of best places to work (Davidson, 2016).

Seven Common Traits of a Best Place to Work

1. **Mission and Values matter**. Mission-driven companies generate higher levels of innovation and better employee retention.
2. **Investment in Culture**. A positive supportive group mentality leads to high levels of employee satisfaction.
3. **Put People First**. In addition to a healthy environment for group coherence, individuals need to be empowered to grow and realize their full potential. The goal is to facilitate staff to bring "their whole selves to work."
4. **Embrace Transparency**. Leading companies are willing to admit to shortfalls and respond openly to criticism and create initiatives with staff for improving operations.
5. **Belief in Career Opportunities**. The best ways to create opportunities for career growth include scheduling regular staff—manager feedback sessions, recognition programs, and sustaining a policy of promoting from within.
6. **Promote Strong Leaders**. Staff rate highly senior leaders who set a positive and inspiring tone in the workplace.
7. **Understand It Is Not All About Pay**. Money may help get a person to join an enterprise, but it is culture and growth opportunities that cultivate long-term satisfaction and job tenure.

These seven outcomes provide guidelines for leadership to develop the best value-creating environment they possibly can. Building unanimity by customizing BARD for your enterprise will contribute to all seven. Now, let us consider five leadership behaviors that more explicitly describe how to facilitate the transformation of your organization.

Leadership for Engagement

With a new level of understanding derived from the Reality Check, the CEO is well positioned to engage key members of the senior management team in a serious and brief discussions. This opportunity for the senior team to share their unique perspectives about the enterprise will entail the CEO using a leadership style that is less directive, one that facilitates discussion through a more interactive Socratic dialogue.

Among the many great books on leadership, one that offers a simple yet useful template for implementing the concepts of this book is *The Leadership Challenge* by Kouzes and Posner (2012). Their research indicates a pattern of five best practices in leadership.

- Inspire a shared vision.
- Model the way.
- Challenge the process.
- Enable others to act.
- Encourage the heart.

Each of the five leadership behaviors from Kouzes and Posner supports the proliferation of BARD throughout the enterprise.

1. **Inspire a Shared Vision**. On the basis of the CEO Reality Check drafts, the Senior System Steward is now properly informed about their personal viewpoint of the organization's VCAs and what they observe as breakdowns within the value streams. This enables one to then document the viewpoints of one's core team, and then after the core team has come to whole-hearted unanimity on what is true and relevant, reach out to other key staff members and stakeholders. The latent wisdom of people, when it comes forth, paints a largely coherent

and comprehensive picture of what is needed to maintain and enhance enterprise value creation for customers. This component helps internalize a shared vision about how to build long-term customer loyalty while lowering Operating Cash Conversion Cycle times.

2. **Model the Way**. Through the Reality Check process and documentation, the CEO walks the talk, that is, leads by example. The CEO reaches out authentically curious to engage the next level of leadership in the adventure starting with the CFO. Each successive inclusion and feeding back with new input inexorably builds unanimity when done respectfully.

3. **Challenge the Process**. By the very nature of BARD, we let data lead the way to what needs to change. By creating safe and productive environments for staff to communicate and act on their tacit knowledge, they will participate in their own regular Reality Checks with one another. This is a platform for significant and impactful change. The transformation toward employee engagement will produce its own long-term benefits when staff get access to relevant data and know how to safely and effectively express their insights.

4. **Enable Others to Act**. BARD contributes to an open, supportive culture with a consistent systems approach, where employees feel enriched by sharing their knowledge and experience, and then seeing their insights integrated into the next iteration of the forward-looking maps for change. By sharing "big picture" financial reports with leaders and key staff, they see more clearly the impact of their activities and how their knowledge can reshape the value sequence as needed.

5. **Encourage the Heart**. Through the simple acts of engaging leaders and staff in effective and regular dialogues about measuring operating activities, a foundation is put in place for significantly enhanced morale and commitment. Measurement of improvements recognizes teams for their accomplishments. People feel it when they know there is sincere interest in knowing and respecting their tacit knowledge of their workplace.

These five leadership principles provide a leadership framework for thoroughly enjoying the implementation of BARD. Through the

CEO's own experience of drafting, that person can then see how to draw their senior team into discovering and affirming their own tacit knowledge through written discovery. It can be a thrilling experience for any leader or staff to see their CEO and CFO valuing their insights, and acting on them.

Engaging the Senior Management Team

It is crucial for the CEO or other Senior System Steward to thoroughly reflect on what they learned in the Reality Check. The KPI and Three-Bottom-Line Metrics are useful to understand the broad-view health of the enterprise. The CEO's Chart of Activities (CoA) draft includes not only a list of the VCAs but also the observed disconnects in the value cycle. After analysis and reflection, the CEO identifies three to five most significant disconnects that need attention to improve results. Then, the CEO thinks through the process of discovering the linkages to the Three Bottom Lines from the 10 Key Internal Financial Drivers.

Now that all the elements of value creation and financial summaries are drafted personally, where and how do we start engaging others?

Begin with the CFO

The Japanese have a word "nimawashi" that translates roughly as "preparing the soil to accept the tree to be successfully transplanted." In a similar way, the BARD approach creates receptivity for the transfer of tacit knowledge. In BARD, the "preparation of the soil" takes the form of a more facilitative leadership approach—moving away from a declarative speaking style to a more Socratic speaking style.

Because the CEO knows his or her own mind on the value creation sequence, she or he can really listen to insights from other people. The best place to start is the CEO's most crucial ally, the CFO. And, the invitation to BARD must be done skillfully to get the desired result. Documenting the way the CFO sees the value creation picture is the starting point for beginning validation of the CEO's initial drafting work. This same approach can be repeated with other senior team members and then cascaded down and across the enterprise.

As the owner of the Chart of Financial Accounts, the CFO is the correct person to first begin considering how to solve the "Missing Methodology," that is, the pervasive need for alignment of business plans with business results, and activities with transactions. This congruence begins by examining the direct connections between specific value-creating operating activities and the financial impacts (on Cash, Profit, and Return) they generate. After the CFO is on-board, the rest of the senior team can be pulled into the mix.

To attract other senior management people into the BARD adventure, we find that the path becomes easier when the CEO asks for feedback and refinements on the joint CEO/CFO draft of the sequence of value-creating activities.

Pulling the CFO and Then Senior Managers into Building the Value Cycle Map

Engagement Step #1: The CFO either reviews the CEO's draft sequence of VCAs (Without disconnects) together, or ideally, if there is time, the CEO invites the CFO to create their own draft (using the same template), and then compare and integrate work products. After each cycle of input, make sure the new input is integrated correctly by checking back with them to affirm the new draft.

Here is an example of a short conversation with the CFO, if time is highly constrained:

Step #1a: Broaching the Subject with the CFO

"Sam, I need your feedback on something. I've created this list as an exercise to understand our company's value creation processes. I spent some time thinking through this crucial question: What is the sequence of VCAs we follow to generate satisfied and loyal customers and all of our consequential financial outcomes? I made a list (19 to 22) of what I see as our most crucial VCAs. I really need your input on this. When do you have 5 to 10 minutes to sit with me to provide your edits?" See partial sample in the left side of Exhibit 5A on p.129. Do not ask for input on the disconnects on the right side until after the CFO's input on the VCAs has been fed back and affirmed. If you ignore this directive, at best, confusion with result.

Commentary on #1a:

Clearly, the most ideal situation would be for the CFO to repeat drafting a CoA just like the CEO did. CFOs may feel that they do not have enough time for another project. So, if there is hesitation to engage in a brainstorm by themselves for 20 minutes by the CFO, a different tactic takes less than 5 minutes and begins with a review of the CEO's documents. This shortcut way of getting feedback on the VCAs draft is the exception to the general BARD guideline to hold back documents until others have completed their own tacit knowledge document. Some of the CFO's tacit knowledge may be overlooked when this shortcut is taken.

Now, to the sample dialogue with CFO when not doing his own CoA brainstorm:

"Here is a clean copy of my first draft of a Chart of Activities. Let us walk through this draft now, and let me know what you see as missing elements from this document. I really need your full deliberate attention on it so I can capture the full story. Among the things I'd like you to evaluate are these:

- What value-creating activities are missing or mis-labeled?
- How would you change the order?
- What sub-activities (not shown here) are so pivotal to our value creation that they need to be added to this list?

After you and I align on our views, then we will be sharing our co-authored document with other members of our senior team in this same manner." Each cycle of input, make sure it is integrated correctly by checking back to affirm the new draft with the full group of contributors so far.

Step #1b: Extending to other Senior Managers

When you subsequently speak to the senior team members, make a similar statement:

"When I have gathered input from all of our senior team, I will create a new version of these documents reflecting the combined insights of everyone. At this point, I ask you to not discuss this project with anyone but me. I want to connect with each person individually without distractions or misconceptions that might come from any side conversations. Can you agree with this approach?"

The idea is to engage senior leaders in practical value cycle analysis at the whole system level one-on-one at first. Sharing tacit knowledge about the sequence of operating activities can give rise to a delighted customer with long-term loyalty to the company's products and services. New collaborators add refinements or missing elements to the analysis. Many leaders will then start to be curious about the tacit job knowledge their own team of people have that can be mined to enrich the conversation.

If at this stage, anyone asks about what you are doing, respond in this vein:

"I am determined to understand deeply how we create value for our customers so we can improve in ways to cultivate customers who have long-term loyalty, because they will be the best possible people to refer new clients. I want to use this approach for both our senior team and, eventually, our whole staff to collaborate on this initiative. When we can arrive at unanimity about core facts of our value streams, then we will have a valid basis for discussing ways to improve our services to customers and stockholders. Does this sound like a practical and fun endeavor?"

On the basis of our decades of experience, we have found that this method of engagement works very well to engage senior management into the BARD adventure.

Engagement Step #2: **Soliciting disconnects and breakdowns**

At end of the draft CoA review with either the CFO or other senior leaders, proceed to the next logical step:

"Based on your review and feedback of my draft CoA, what would you say are the two to four most serious issues where you see there is a significant problem within our operating activities that is interfering with VCAs and value throughput?"

One of the main purposes of this dialogue is to begin demonstrating the art of positing a good problem statement. When we eventually implement the engagement and alignment process with an entire enterprise, we ask many dozens of people to answer in writing this question at the same time: "What two to four things drives you the craziest every day, that you know are costing the enterprise money, and/or the end-customer value they could otherwise receive?"

In Chapter 2 on disconnects, we discussed the importance of framing disconnects in a positively stated form. Here are some examples of a negatively stated problem and a semantically positive reframing of it.

Examples of creating positive phrasing about value disconnects:

- "Not enough boundaries with our clients" becomes instead "Customization for clients entered into too lightly."
- "Lack of Marketing Plan definition" can become "Market targets and access points need more definition."
- "Poor requirements definition" becomes "Strong drivers to better define requirements such as. . . ."

Options for evoking alignment on Disconnects:

1. Ideally, when the CFO (or other senior managers) expresses a disconnect in very general or negative phrasing, one can request that they rephrase it in semantically positive terms. And ask for more precise phrasing if it appears to be a generalization. For example, if the disconnect is phrased as "bad communication," then with proper feedback and a request for more specific phrasing, you might get a revised expression like this: "The marketing team that generates prospects and the sales team that closes prospects are not consistently exchanging crucial information to close new business."

2. If time or other constraints are present, then the shortcut would be to use your best interpretation of the phrasing and convert it into a semantically positive statement, and then verify with them that it captures their disconnect insights. This second option is a step down in terms of engagement, and may lose insights that could be gained if the leader is willing to reflect more on supporting the other to clarify and reword the disconnect themselves.

Accordingly, this is how the CEO's Reality Check can be cascaded down and through the organization by iterating and synthesizing the working documents in such a way as to create a new, more powerful Management Operating System documents and maps.

To summarize our approach: First, we take the input from the CEO and CFO, and then use their work product to engage other senior team members in developing unanimity about VCAs. From that unanimity and alignment, the agreement-building method is replicated. The CEO and CFO, as a now genuinely unified team, invite their two to five key direct reports into exactly the same process, thereby dialing in unanimity and alignment among the half dozen or so crucial people supporting all the domains of the Value Creation Cycle.

We must consistently reinforce the mandate that, after using a CoA draft to get edits on that shared documents, none of the new circle members are to show their work products to anyone who has not contributed their own personal work. If a more senior or influential person shows their written or verbal thoughts with someone over whom they have authority, then the subordinate person may be likely to modify their conclusions to fit better with their perception of their superior's view. In other words, after using their draft CoA as the conversation starter on value creation, and as the knowledge mining proceeds, leaders must be hypervigilant not to pollute another colleague's tacit knowledge before they have a chance to share their hard-won knowledge in writing or in the form of notes taken during a focused conversation.

Engagement Step #3: Solicit System KPI candidates

After the disconnects are tight and you as CEO have revised your initial documents from the Reality Check, the next question to the CFO and then each Senior Team members is this:

"Now that you have identified these activity disconnects, I'd like to get clear about what you think is the primary place in the value creation sequence each of your disconnects first impacts the value cycle sequence?"

After the two or three disconnects have been linked to its VCAs Account, then it should be numbered alongside its corresponding VCA on the CoA with Disconnects. See Exhibit 5A on p.129 MACPA CoA and Disconnects for the matching of activities and breakdowns.

After the VCAs are lined up with related disconnects, the next key question can be asked of each person in a next very brief and focused meeting.

"What are the one to two key nonfinancial data points (avoid use of the term 'metric' at this time) that we could possibly measure and track to determine either the cost of the disconnect in this activity, or how, if we have been trying to improve it, we can measure whether actual activities improvement has occurred? Through what numbers could we know if we have improved the value-creating activity?"

Gather information from each person in short and focused 5-minute face-to-face conversations on each disconnect question at hand.

During these brief discussions, remember to do the following:

- Carefully take notes.
- Restate that what is occurring is simply a brainstorming session.
- Avoid any debate about the merit of the ideas offered.
- Ask only clarifying questions.
- Move rapidly to conclusion.
- Use active feedback by restating what the CFO (and then each of the senior leaders) say, as you confirm notes of their input, being certain they are checked for accuracy.

Now that a third iteration to harvest the tacit knowledge is documented (showing the list of activities first, and related disconnects in the next column to the right), create the next more refined version of the KPIs in relation to the VCAs and identify any disconnects. Then, offer the revised Reality Check documents to those in the circle so they can see how the discussion is revealing and enriching a more holistic view and add any insights.

In a group meeting, drill down to gain at least consensus, if not unanimity, on the relevant few KPIs that are crucial at this time. Once they are validated to be accurate and useful over multiple periods, these can become the master measures staff will all be tracking and refining going forward. All these work products are the foundation for spreading BARD methods to additional leaders, and initial key staff.

Jeff Lueken, CEO, Lueken's Food Stores, Reflects on Importance of Engaging Tacit Knowledge

In reference to the book *Deep Smarts*, I have understood and personally experienced the Reality Check process to be an effective method of documenting tacit knowledge and getting people to analyze, organize, and qualify their own understanding of the business. This is an outcome of the value-creating activity analysis. The quote I like from Tom Hood is specific to this outcome, when he asks how to get the staff to "understand and engage". These two key words are on the minds of virtually every executive, including myself, in relation to what I want from my 400 employee owners. The Chart of Activities helps qualify the business, and the breadth of enterprise knowledge, then the three bottom lines quantify it.

Chapter Summary and Conclusions

During this chapter, we focused on how to set up the proper tone to foster the receptivity of the senior leadership team for BARD methods. Unless you follow the recommended step-by-step procedures, you may find less than optimal receptivity and subsequently weaker unanimity from the senior team.

We examined how Kouzes and Posner's Leadership paradigm appropriately empowers the CEO to earn the cooperation and support of senior leaders to transform the organization into a high-performing enterprise. You learned how all of their five leadership behaviors are inherently cultivated by BARD.

Finally, we revealed how to pull senior leadership gradually into a meaningful dialogue toward collaboration on what matters most—sustaining and improving Value Creation. All leadership development programs that succeed move ahead when the entire senior team is committed to long-term change, and have both the skills and the discipline to model the way for other leaders and staff to follow.

When senior managers are "on board" and fully aligned with the CEO in whole-hearted unanimity on the facts, the power of that ever-growing unanimity is unleashed through continued inclusion of colleagues that know value. Coherence and clear focus propel the enterprise toward higher levels of achievement and operating excellence in delivering value to customers.

In Chapter 6, you will see how to develop a habit of effective meetings called "huddles" to sustain enthusiasm for continuous improvements.

References

Davidson, K. (2016). "A Best Workplace Takes Hard Work." *Workface* 95, no. 6, p.26.

Kouzes, J., and Posner, B. (2012). *The Leadership Challenge: How to Make Extraordinary Things Happen in Organizations.* 5th edition. San Francisco, CA: Jossey-Bass.

CHAPTER 6

Monitor and Report Performance

Ballard's Alignment and Reporting Disciplines

1. *Map and Identify*: Map the sequence of VCAs; identify disconnects.
2. *Analyze and Project*: Three-bottom-line analysis with rolling cash flow projections.
3. *Define and Link*: Define financial drivers and disconnects; develop key KPIs linking activities and transactions.
4. *Engage and Align*: Engage leaders and staff by aligning on both true core facts and desired outcomes.
5. *Monitor and Report*: Regularly monitor performance in periodic huddles using outcome-driven agendas.

In this chapter, you will see how to use regular, effectively run "huddles" to promote forward momentum toward creating a fully aligned senior team—one that is committed to achieving value creation excellence. Kremer's four questions will serve as the guiding template for each huddle session. Use them to establish a sturdy foundation for senior leadership to develop unanimity on fundamental value creation. That unanimity will serve as the basis for working in alignment to discover, establish, and test the organization's most critical key performance indicators (KPIs).

The BARD prescription:

- Make it a high priority to document the current, yet unrecorded, enterprise knowledge that is held by senior managers and their teams.

- Develop the shared skills and discipline to collectively apply the empirical process (scientific method) at work to develop and validate master measures.
- Track your progress toward reaching benchmarks.
- Meet regularly as the core leadership group to build whole-hearted unanimity by honing measurement skills and reinforcing team alignment.

Huddle Meetings to Sustain Improvement Efforts

To create continuing momentum for BARD, your first task will be to create a small working group of senior managers, the Decision Team (DT), to develop unanimity on high-priority intentions for improving business operations. This senior team meets monthly for at least several rounds to establish alignment and momentum for continuous improvement efforts. The monthly meetings are called "huddles" in the spirit of a sport's team reviewing results and deciding the next play(s).

In the book *Managing by the Numbers*, author and software innovator Chuck Kremer spelled out his approach to managing the plethora of possible projects any senior team deals with. In custom learning engagements with Fortune 2,000 clients, including some with Jahn Ballard, Kremer taught a four-question sequence for effectively managing senior team focus on managing by their numbers. Evolving toward measurement excellence, the DT habituates itself to work through Kremer's four questions sequentially in each performance huddle to build a foundation of unanimity.

Kremer's Four Questions for Building Unanimity

Q1: Which of the three bottom lines is weakest?

Q2: Which key drivers impacts that bottom line?

Q3: What is the business story behind the driver and its impact on the bottom line?

Q4: What are the most important things that need attention to correct disconnects?

Q1: Which of the three bottom lines is weakest?

The three bottom lines are profit, cash flow from operations, and return on asset stewardship. Which one of the three deviates most from expectations? Just the one that most deviates may be sufficient, or more depth analysis may be called for.

To evaluate **profitability**, it may be helpful to compare Return on Sales (ROS) percentage compared to other companies in the industry. Often, there will be an industry association that can provide such data. Be careful about comparing your organization's ROS to the industry average because that standard is mediocrity, that is, the average. Frequently, your target might be the upper quartile for the industry.

Let us look at some sample data. Assume your ROS is 5 percent. The industry data provide three numbers: lower quartile (2.5 percent), mean (5.5 percent), and upper quartile (8.0 percent), which indicates that 75 percent of respondents had ROS below 8.0 percent. If you aspire to be "average," the current performance is slightly below average. If instead you aspire to be one of the top 25 percent in the industry on this metric, there is much improvement needed.

Cash Flow from Operating Activities or Operating Cash Flow (OCF)

If deviation from internal goals is not sufficient to make the call, then again industry comparables may be helpful. OCF can be found on the Cash Flow Statement of any publicly traded company, and almost always in the Indirect Format, and therefore not revealing the changes to actual cash accounts. Instead of looking at the dollar amount for comparison, consider the idea of calculating Cash Flow from Operating Activities per common share. This is calculated by taking Cash Flow from Operating Activities and dividing by the average number of common shares outstanding during the year. Without specific detailed data on what shares may have been issued or repurchased during the year, it is acceptable to simply add the beginning shares plus ending shares . . . and then divide by two.

But, what happens when you cannot find industry data? In such a case, if you work in an industry with publicly traded companies, most competitors will have published financial statements audited by Certified

Public Accountants (CPAs). These are public documents that you can obtain through the competitor's website or through the SEC Form 10-K. All three bottom lines can be calculated easily from a competitor's financial statements.

Proceed cautiously in making comparisons to public companies because many of these firms are diversifying their family of subsidiaries by integrating vertically or by acquiring firms in different industries. In such cases, the calculations of competitor metrics may be skewed away from a pure calculation in a specific industry.

Return on Asset stewardship is an easily obtained number for public companies too. As you may recall, this percentage is calculated by dividing Average Total Assets into Net Income. It shows the rate of return earned by management on the asset capacity base available to them. If there is a weakness in ROA, then, you may want to look to the DuPont Formula to break down the math into smaller components to identify root causes of poor performance as in example above.

After identifying which bottom line needs attention most, then it is time to drill down to identify the drivers that affect the roll-up of numbers for that bottom line.

Q2: Which key drivers impacts that bottom line?

In Chapter 4 we laid out how 10 internal drivers create the three-bottom-line results. Some of the drivers directly create the profit bottom line. Other drivers create cash flow from operating activities. Leading inquiry to discover which are which, and then which VCAs impact them, can lead to significant refinement in a KPI's usefulness. Check out Exhibit 4A on p.127, the Maryland Association of Certified Public Accountants (MACPA) actuals from 1998 to 2011 and 2012 Pro Formas for a multiyear view of key financial driver and bottom-line trending. See Exhibit 6C on p.132 for an Activity to Results Flow Chart from 2011 showing a few sample linkages of key drivers to financial outcomes.

To gain insights about how data is trending, it is often useful to conduct separate horizontal common-size statement analysis of both the income statement and the direct method cash flow statement. In common-size analysis the base year data become the denominator of a percentage that shows how each subsequent year's data are changing with respect to the base year. For example, see the table below that shows a four-year sequence of sales revenue.

Year	Sales Revenue	% of Base
Year 1	$4,000,000	0
Year 2	$4,400,000	10
Year 3	$5,000,000	25
Year 4	$6,000,000	50

By creating an income statement with columns showing the current year and the past few years, it is often obvious where there are problems. Of course, it is important to realize that some expenses by their nature are largely fixed or variable. The assessment of changes should consider a judgment about the underlying nature of the cost type.

In a similar manner, you can create a time series (four or five-year array) of the key driver metrics to see what is trending negatively. This will begin to narrow the focus on what needs attention.

Q3: What is the business story behind the driver and its impact on the bottom line?

The MACPA Value Cycle Map with KPI Loops (Exhibit 6C on p.132) shows how a Value Cycle Map can display draft or validated master measures so the linkage from activity to bottom line is established through the disconnect, KPI, and key driver. The senior team can draft their version of the value map, consider linkages at test huddles, and come together on where they need more insight on operating activities for their unanimity to continue growing.

Unpacking the business story behind the decline in a key driver ultimately may be best discovered by engaging people on the front line, who do the value-creating work every day. They are positioned to provide insights, and can be motivated to drill down into the data and procedures to discover alternative solutions for improving performance. The tacit knowledge of employees is one of the most valuable assets an organization possesses. Engaging employees to reveal their observations and wisdom through years of experience can create significant new value. However, it is important to establish an environment that encourages effective collaboration, and does not stir up fear. Sometimes, employees are hesitant to share what they know because they are concerned it may cause them to lose their jobs, or jobs of their friends. In Lean Management initiatives it is common practice to state clearly that no one will lose their job because of the efficiencies gained from lean projects.

Q4: What are the most important things that need attention to correct disconnects?

Even within a specifically defined project (e.g., to reduce processing time on an activity), there may be several possible approaches or ways of doing business that need repair or elimination. Usually, the list of priorities begins with low-cost, quickly implemented changes and then progresses toward those changes that will produce the most impact on the objectives of the project.

Steps for aligning the Decision Team's work:

1. **The DT starts by organizing the total set of problems in the enterprise and defining where in the value cycle each breakdown begins.** The Reality Check documentation has already created the list of breakdowns in the value creation sequence, which we call "disconnects" because they almost always occur in hand-offs occurring either upstream or downstream of a VCA. With this list already in place, the DT can define which VCA is the beginning point of each disconnect, or constraining influence. This occurs by locating each disconnect on the sequence of Value-Creating Activities where it begins to influence the VCA(s). Sometimes this can be accomplished by following the sequence through the written descriptions of VCAs. Sometimes it may require flowcharting to see more clearly.

   Then, the team is prepared to **begin considering the workflow measurement(s) most relevant to identify and mitigate root causes of poor performance.** As and if needed the senior team in their pilot phase draw on in-house experts (usually from the shop floor or other grassroots levels). Sometimes data collection is required to clarify the disconnect situations. At this point, move cautiously to engage people at different levels into the BARD adventure. It is ideal for the DT to do this big picture work on its own first, so as to get its collective "head on straight," before attempting to mine the tacit job knowledge from the larger body of leaders and staff. If the DT is not thoroughly on the same page in its own collective mind, with a body of documented whole-hearted unanimity, the risks of not reaching full staff unanimity and alignment on activities moving forward are significantly increased. If it is necessary to engage others in the initial framing and measurement collaboration, they should be invited to assist in the same manner as the CEO invited the CFO, that is, in a manner that slowly wakes up other leaders and staff to consider the value creation sequence. Asking for written information in a highly focused manner works best to begin collaboration. Sometimes, a very short face-to-face meeting may be ideal for most rapid note taking of key insights. Avoid at this stage disclosing the larger purpose of the DT's work until it can be done in the most integrated manner. During an upgrade, we operate strictly on a "need-to-know" basis in order to reduce risk of wobbles.

2. The **senior team invents candidate system-level KPIs** that they believe will definitely show when results have improved. Think carefully about what measurements will best reveal anticipated changes to costs or effectiveness of the VCAs. Brainstorming is often a useful exercise to challenge people's unrestricted creativity on this issue. KPI data should be presented in a one-page visual summary, so that key data can then be extracted to become part of any regularly updated and monitored one-page scoreboards or dashboards. When the desired level of performance improvement has been achieved, this may indicate the need to transition attention toward a different disconnect, or validating it as an ongoing master measure.

3. By examining the KPIs developed, combined with documents from the DT's Reality Check, the team then **chooses three to five high-priority measures** for improving the value-creating results of the enterprise. The team will be periodically updating this list as breakdowns are fixed and new priorities come to the surface. This cycle naturally becomes part of the continuous way of doing business for the DT.

4. **The senior team agrees on who will do what and when.** At any point of time, the next steps could involve:
   - Mapping a process to better understand the variables and workflow
   - Collecting baseline data on the current state of a process or variable
   - Searching for best practices on a specific process
   - Organizing a small kaizen (continuous improvement) team for intensive problem-solving

Before dispersing, the senior team should agree on a time for the next meeting (usually 2 to 4 weeks later) and remind each person they are expected to report on a one-page Activity Statement. The activity measures and tasks should be documented and circulated to all DT members shortly after the meeting as a reminder of what is expected from each person, and then resent shortly before the next meeting. When a time comes for other staff to invent and propose their Activity Statement versions, the seniors team's test versions add great reference points.

The fundamental model of value-creating activities, disconnects, and candidate system KPIs is ever more unanimously affirmed by the DT as it conducts ongoing periodic "huddles" and measurement integration meetings. Huddles are similar to what a disciplined football team accomplishes in just a few seconds in their huddle between plays, which are able to occur on the field in real time because of the unanimity and alignment generated by practice and discussions off the field as preparations for games.

Huddle Meetings should be no shorter than 30 to 45 minutes, and no longer than 75 to 90 minutes. Progress on each of the master measures (three to five candidate system KPIs) will be reported in one-page summary format so that fast and effective analysis and feedback can be given. The next set of action steps are agreed in the huddles and documented for follow-up at the next huddle.

Revised Value Cycle Map

After the DT decides on the three to five most important improvement measures and projects toward enhancing the value-creating activities, the Value Cycle Map introduced in Chapter 2 (see Exhibit 2B on p.116) can be enhanced. We present the revised map for MACPA in Exhibit 6C on p.132 as Value Cycle Map with KPI Loops.

Note that the Value Cycle Map portrays MACPA's 19 core Value-Creating Activities Accounts in a clockwise circular array beginning with "engage potential members." As a highly visible organizational artifact, the map functions as a constant reminder about how the association provides value to their 9,000 CPA members statewide.

Notice the numbered KPI Loops in upper right (#5), upper left (#1), and lower right (#6) corners. These numbers refer to the VCA Accounts identified as containing significant breakdowns that needed high-priority correction.

The leadership and staff identified VCA #5 (Seminars, Conferences, Chapters, and Webcasts) as a key activity with a consistently serious disconnect (Missed Revenue Targets). The KPI activity data measures developed by the staff included both a behavioral element (Shortfall in Projected Attendance) and a related financial measure (Seminar Revenue Budget). Finally, the KPI Loop reminded everyone that the related driver, Cost of Goods Sold divided by Revenues, affects the Net Profit Bottom Line.

As a second example, consider the story behind the KPI Loop in the lower right corner, which was related to VCA #6 "Customized Learning Solutions." MACPA was the largest provider of custom AICPA (American Institute of CPAs) learning events for Fortune 100 finance departments. The leadership and staff team had gathered information indicating a breakdown in the billing cycle for that income center. The team decided that the relevant KPI coupled the activities element (Number of Days to Submit a validated list of attendees for invoicing) and the related financial measures (% of Dollars Owed and # of Days Outstanding Receivable). This KPI affected both the Income Statement and Cash Statement, through the prime key driver (Operating Cash Flow divided by Sales) and affected the second bottom line (OCF).

The revised Value Cycle Map with KPI Loops (Exhibits 6C on p.132) helped keep everyone at MACPA focused on the most important tasks at hand, that is, tackling improvement efforts identified in the three KPI Loops. Huddles typically begin with a quick (3–5 min) review of rolling Pro Formas (Exhibits 6B and 4A on p.127) showing results since the previous period, then visual examination of the Value Cycle Map (Exhibit 2E on p.119 and Exhibits B and C on p.137 in Appendices for samples) key VCAs, disconnects and measures (Exhibit 6C) as the agenda progresses through the four questions. In the last 10 minutes, review material assumptions (Exhibit 4B on p.128) underlying the rolling Pro Formas (Exhibits 6B and 4A on p.127) in light of the discussions, and then confirm team meetings and next huddle dates and times.

Guidelines for Successful Huddle Meetings:
- Define the meeting outcomes collaboratively well ahead of the event, then build the agenda.
- Using the combined set of outcomes, establish a draft statement of intent (one sentence) for the meeting, and get alignment by going back and forth until there is complete agreement.
- Develop meeting agenda draft and iterate items and sequence only after the first two steps are complete.
- Publish the agenda 24 to 72 hours before the meeting, with all relevant data for the meeting attached, especially the one-page activities summaries. Avoid changes to agenda in the last 24 hours if possible.
- KPI owners and/or teams are expected to submit the one-page activity statements (See Exhibits A, B, and C in Appendices for samples) indicating new data since the previous huddle. This expectation should be clearly communicated and agreed upon before ending the huddle.

KPI Owner or Team Meeting Outcomes

- Review KPI impact. Compare actual data to expected improvement levels to share on a one page Activity Statement.
- Hear team reports on recent activity measures, including measures of disconnects thwarting progress.
- Agree on next iterations of refined activities measuring, and KPI definitions.
- Within the three to five master measures, continue with more detailed surfacing of bottlenecks or other factors hindering cash flow, productivity, and effectiveness.
- Summarize with the take-away insights gained about operating activities.

Short-term Improvement Projects Tracking

Exhibit 6A on p.130 is a real sample of a data mining company's Improvement Tracking Report that is organized by three columns from left to right showing:

- A list of the high-priority projects named by value-creating activities (VCA) that need improvement
- A description of the specific breakdowns identified within the VCAs
- A list of agreed-upon KPIs that initially serve to collect baseline data and subsequently to monitor progress of improvement efforts

Multiyear Operations Finance Tracking

Exhibit 6B on p.131 provides an example of MACPA's big-picture one-page report that was developed over a period of years to track progress on improving profits and cash flow from operations. This report was generated through the Financial Scoreboard software—demo available at www.businessexpertpress.com/books/mastering-leadership-alignment-linking-value-creation-cash-flow.

Summary observations on Exhibit 6B reflecting on BARD impacts on period 2001 to 2011:

- Around 1996 MACPA was headed toward insolvency.
- In 1996, new CEO from private industry, Tom Hood, takes over.
- 2001 begins BARD Management Operating System Upgrade; OCF improves—at $4 million in sales revenue, cash from operating activities improves $971,000.
- Profits rise to breakeven and beyond in 2002 and 2003.
- In 2003 to 2004, MACPA software system crashes at the crucial point in billing cycle; Profit continues to rise and OCF turns slightly negative.
- In 2004 to 2005, software problem solved; OCF recovers. Profit improvement tracks for five straight years with revenue growth.
- In 2007 to 2008, MACPA invests in sales growth; net profit declines as planned; sales go up.
- In 2008 to 2010, economy crashes; sales remain high, OCF and Net Profit plummet; both recover by 2010.
- In 2010 and 2011, sales and OCF remain high. Net Profit highest ever.

This specific one-page report was iteratively updated each year as MACPA strove to stabilize both profits and cash flow from operations. It kept the management team's eye squarely on how to address each challenge. Except for the dislocations caused by the financial crisis in 2008 to 2009, MACPA tracked a steady path of improving business effectiveness through BARD methods.

BARD Cultivates Cash Flow

No enterprise can last for decades unless it tends toward growing cash flow from operations at least as fast, if not faster, than it is growing profit. How do you use BARD to do just that?

When implemented correctly, BARD has produced significantly positive gains in cash flow from operations within the first year. Three companies (with annual sales from $4million to $68 million) that used BARD have reported an average increase of 79 percent in OCF within that first year, with an average year-one cash improvement over one million dollars. These incredibly significant jumps in OCF show a pattern—that using BARD has the effect of revitalizing and re-invigorating enterprise activities and results.

In an effort to leverage the full cash flow improvement potential, there may be a need to extend the BARD methodology both horizontally to other business units and vertically to shop floor levels of the enterprise. Doing that will require additional tools for proper collaborative planning, implementation, and institutionalization. For example, when you engage employees at customer-facing levels, they can uncover many opportunities for streamlining business processes and eliminating waste. In fact, there may be more process improvement projects than can be done at the same time. So, it will be important to work with their subject matter knowledge to determine what projects are most important. This requires both experience with the Reality Check and also group facilitation skills.

Jeff Lueken, CEO, Lueken's Food Stores, Reflects on Revising the Value Cycle Map

Delineating the understanding of the business into four domains makes the process more manageable. Some people have greater knowledge in one area, and so it also lends itself to approaching this more systematically. This process also transitions people from the mindset of "we have problems" to one of articulation and eventually a solution. It also removes 'the fog' that many times covers ongoing problems that have never been addressed, and therefore become part of the daily noise that is simply ignored. They can become front and center.

The resulting Value Cycle Map is revealing. In one sense, it's inspiring for me to see a visual representation of the shared knowledge; of what everyone here does to create value. At the same time, it can be daunting to fully understand all of these facets and come to the realization that all of them aren't being delivered at the same level.

Conclusion and Summary

On the basis of the CEO's successfully "pulling" engagement with other senior leaders, the foundation for legitimate, comprehensive, long-term enterprise transformation has been properly cultivated. Many organizational development programs fail before they get started because top management is not 100 percent committed to the new direction. Commitment goes beyond lip service support. It must be modeled by the senior team showing they are doing the new methods themselves, and also by engaging the next layers of staff while attempts to measure activities and results effectively continue.

In the next chapter, we go deeper into understanding value streams and cycles. Then in the last chapter we step back and review the comprehensive picture of how BARD wakes up step-by-step management awareness to fully aligned, fully unanimous picture of coherent agreement about how to steer the enterprise to operational and financial excellence.

CHAPTER 7

Value Stream and Value Cycle Accounting

Ballard's Alignment and Reporting Disciplines

1. *Map and Identify*: Map the sequence of VCAs; identify disconnects.
2. *Analyze and Project*: Three-bottom-line analysis with rolling cash flow projections.
3. *Define and Link*: Define financial drivers and disconnects; develop key KPIs linking activities and transactions.
4. *Engage and Align*: Engage leaders and staff by aligning on both true core facts and desired outcomes.
5. *Monitor and Report*: Regularly monitor performance in periodic huddles using outcome-driven agendas.

As part of the upgrade to your Management Operating System (MOS) emerging from BARD thinking, it may be helpful to reflect on how your financial reports are generated. As enterprises move toward transforming into a high-performing business, it will be important for financials to assist the monitoring of operating activities progress in achieving new priorities.

Traditional accounting systems typically do not provide managers with the data they need to effectively monitor progress on new MOS business priorities. However, most accounting systems can be mapped to provide both Generally Accepted Accounting Principles (GAAP) financial statements as well as any specially designed internal reports. Note that for internal reports there are no official rules; data can be defined and arrayed according to the needs of decision makers. An organization focused on optimizing value-creating activities will often benefit from some form of Lean Value Stream Accounting that brings attention to specific operational/financial objectives and encourages "crew" behaviors that promote more efficient value-creating activities.

Lean Accounting is described officially in the 42-page Statement on Management Accounting issued by the American Institute of Management Accountants in the document *Accounting for the Lean Enterprise: Major Changes to the Accounting Paradigm* (IMA, 2006). Lean Accounting is appropriate for organizations that have adopted Lean Management principles derived from the Toyota Production System shop floor practices. Lean Management is now a generic model for continuous process improvements that consists of elements, rules, and tools. The primary focus is on maximizing value creation for the benefit of customers according to their expectations. The BARD model is a Lean Management methodology, enhancing long-term customer loyalty, streamlining business processes, and supporting committed, engaged employees who actively utilize their inherent knowledge to drive the organization toward excellence.

What Is a Value Stream?

Think of a Value Stream as the sequence of activities dedicated to producing a single product or service line. The value stream begins with assessment of customer needs and then also spans product design/development, manufacturing of the product, shipping, and customer service including warranty service. In an organization that is dedicated to lean methods similar to BARD, optimization of value streams is a permanently cycling collaboration, which we recommend be in concert with a Direct Format Cash Statement.

In this chapter we examine the advantages for decision makers that come from a Lean Value Stream approach to producing financial statements, especially income statements, which illuminate the results of operating activities.

First, let us consider how Value Stream Income Statements are different from traditionally prepared income statements. We chose the example of a manufacturing company because the Income Statement tends to be more complex than a service enterprise, any of which can apply these methods as well manufacturing.

Characteristics of a Value Stream Income Statement Approach for Manufacturing Enterprises

- **Assign as many personnel as possible to work exclusively for one value stream.** In this way, the vast majority of costs are assigned instead of allocated to product families based on some arbitrary basis. Usually, with some creative training approaches, 80 to 85 percent of personnel can be assigned. Imagine a three-person marketing team consisting of a director and two specialists, one focused on social media and the other on print and radio media. If the two specialists train each other to become generalists, then they can be assigned to be 100 percent dedicated to one single-value stream group. The director of marketing would still be a dotted line reporting authority, but the marketing reps would have direct reporting responsibility to the Value Stream Manager. The Director's salary and benefits would continue to be an Administrative Operating Expense (common cost) but the compensation of the marketing reps would show as an expense of the Value Stream to which they are assigned. In this manner, the silos of operating expenses are distributed by operating activities, and much of this cost is no longer a general/administrative operating expense.

- **Extend the range of a value stream backwards and forwards from factory operations**. Any value stream begins with product development and ends with customer service. The entire stream touches many functional areas including marketing, sales, supply chain, inventory control, production, shipping, accounting, and customer service. Ideally, personnel from all these functional areas become fully dedicated to the value stream focus on maximizing value to customers. The synergy of the newly aligned Value Cycle Map is powerful in changing behaviors and focus on results within each value stream.

- **Emphasize actual incurred costs instead of absorption costing (GAAP)**. Traditional manufacturing accounting utilizes full absorption costing, which means that as units of inventory are manufactured, costs are accumulated in finished inventory accounts that consist of the cost of materials, labor, and overhead. When units are sold, costs move out of the Inventory account into an expense account called Cost of Goods Sold. Thus, if some units are manufactured but not sold, then the costs of those units sit in the asset account (Finished Goods Inventory) until they are sold.

Lean-focused manufacturers want to reduce inventory levels as part of their priorities to eliminate waste and improve operating cash flow. In some cases, they may prepare internal income statements that assign all incurred costs to each value stream . . . even if some units are not sold. This will reduce both raw materials overstocking and overproduction of finished goods, which mistakenly is often encouraged by incentive systems that reward plant managers for minimizing unit costs.

- **All expenditures for acquiring raw materials for manufacturing or finished goods for resale are charges against current revenues.** The goal is to create incentives for value stream managers to create just-in-time supply chain relationships where overstocking of inventory is avoided.

- **Value Stream Margin (instead of Profit) is the basis for evaluating the effectiveness of product or service lines and should be the basis for compensation incentives.** In many operations, operations managers are rewarded for minimizing unit costs, which sounds good but often leads to undesirable behaviors. For example, it is well known among manufacturing managers that the way to reduce unit costs is to overproduce and thereby spread fixed overhead manufacturing costs over a larger number of units. Unsold inventory is cash sitting on a shelf in a warehouse, which is just a form of waste.

- **Isolate special case costs for monitoring.** For example, if the company has stated priorities for reducing scrap and rework, these costs should be tracked and shown separately so results can be compared to goals.

With this overview of how Lean Value Stream Income Statements are different from traditional absorption costing statements required by US-GAAP, let us examine a specific sample of such a document. Let us assume we are running a business called Spinning Wheel Bikes, a manufacturer of two lines of bicycles: street bikes and mountain bikes. The company uses absorption costing income statements for public reporting on the basis of generally accepted auditing standards. But, for internal purposes, Spinning Wheel Bikes has developed its own system of management reporting for profit-making activities based on the methods described above.

Spinning Wheel Bikes: Sample Value Stream Income Statement

See Exhibit 7A on p.133 Spinning Wheels Bikes (SWB) for 2015. A Template for Exhibit 7A can be requested at/change url to www .MOSupgrade.com/MLA/Library. This statement provides data for a clear evaluation of Value Stream leaders' effectiveness based on these features for each value stream:

- All incurred costs for Materials, Labor, and Overhead are assigned to each value stream even if some of the units are unsold at the end of the period. These costs can be found in the Control Accounts for each of the three input categories. This procedure encourages managers to avoid overstocking of raw materials by negotiating just-in-time supply chain agreements.
- At SWB, managers are not rewarded for minimizing unit costs. Instead, they are rewarded by reducing both raw materials and finished goods inventories, *and* for maximizing value stream profits, *and* for reducing the costs of poor quality.
- Costs of Quality are isolated to keep each value stream team focused on reducing the percentage of each of these categories. Targets are updated annually. Notice that the

rework costs for Mountain Bikes are 3.7 percent of net sales revenue compared to only 1.7 percent for Street Bikes.

- Notice how much of operating expenses are no longer considered as common costs. Much of the magnitude of common costs are now assigned to each value stream. Much of the earlier combined common costs are now assigned to value streams.

- Changes in ending inventory (at absorption costing from GAAP statements not shown here) are indicated by percentage changes from 2014 year end to 2015 year end. Both value streams have *reduced* ending finished goods inventory levels (3.2 and 6.8 percent, respectively), whereas raw material inventories have *increased* (7.2 and 1.4 percent, respectively).

- SWB made changes to its Chart of Accounts so that they are now aligned to the Value-Creating Activities developed through BARD. This realignment allows the Decision Team and staff impact measurement team down the road to harvest relevant data for their streamlining and other improvement projects. As an example, find the sales activities detailed costs shown in Exhibit 7B on p.135 showing both the direct activities and support needed to drive business revenue generation. Notice the breakdown of the total sales expense line in the Income Statement into cost incurred by Street and Mountain product families. When the percentage breakdown is added to enhance this report, managers can evaluate similarities and differences of cost incurrence across the product families. In the Exhibit 7B example, notice that the sum of percentages for base salaries and commissions for closing sales adds to 65 percent of total costs for each family. This suggests a consistent pattern of compensation for sales people across the enterprise value streams.

- Value-Creating Domain categories (presented in Chapter 2) are shown on the left side according to the legend shown. This reinforces the all-inclusive territory of the four domains, that is, all accounts in the income statement can be categorized into one of the four domains.

The Charge. As part of your re-examination of everything your organization does to create value for customers, consider how the realignment of your accounting reports can help shape positive employee behaviors and assist in the development of financial incentives for managers consistent with lean objectives.

More precisely, we recommend that the enterprise's financials and Chart of Accounts be reframed in the context of "behaviorals" in the form of a Chart of Activities drafted during the first step of BARD, described in Chapter 2. Such realignment of the account categories will allow the organization to more coherently accumulate the costs of each value-creating activity.

Accounting's Missing Piece of the Puzzle

As described in Chapter 2, a validated Chart of Activities can emerge as a valuable model for reorienting the traditional Chart of Accounts toward an enterprise focus, by listing in correct sequence the value-creating activities that precede any transaction. But, in most enterprises the accounting system does not mirror this logic. Usually Charts of Accounts are based on the layout of the financial statements instead of the needs of management or the pattern of value-creating activities.

Accounting is a method of recording and presenting all the transactions in an organization for any given period of time or date. Accountants use a double-entry system for recording all transactions, first in a Journal, which is like a diary of chronological transactions. Then, the same data are classified by type of account category in the General Ledger. At the end of an accounting period, adjusting entries are made to conform to the accrual system required by GAAP. Then, transaction summaries known as financial statements are prepared: Balance Sheet, Income Statement, and Cash Flow Statements where the Indirect Format is required by US GAAP FASB #95, and the little-used Direct Cash Format often lays hidden as an option, applied by few enterprises. The Direct Method provides more understandable information to operating leaders. We strongly favor the Direct Method for internal use as the compliment to the Value Stream Income Statement.

When an enterprise commits to aligning Senior Teams according to Ballard's methods, its senior team will discover a naturally growing desire to see financial information formatted to be consistent with the sequential activities descriptions available in the list of Value-Creating Activities. In most accounting systems, the Controller can arrange for the internal Income Statement to be mapped so that the accounts are accumulated into the four activity domains:

- Market segmentation/prospect identification (marketing activities)
- Customer acquisition (selling activities)
- Customer delivery sequence (activities for production of goods and services)
- Back office support (administrative and general service activities)

Ballard Method leaders seek a congruent system for reporting data in their internal operational and financial statements. Instead of the classic Chart of Accounts, which is typically an alphabetical list of the names of accounts that appear on detailed balance sheet (cash, marketable securities, receivables, inventory, and so on) and the income statement (beginning with revenue accounts and then expenses), if we choose, we can now reorganize our thinking about the list of financial accounts according to the Chart of Activities.

In making such a change to context of the Chart of Accounts, we signal again to everyone inside the organization that we are driven by the sequence of value-creating activities we follow to generate satisfied and loyal, if not thrilled and delighted, customers.

Bargerstock's Value Stream Income Statement

Observe the new organization of the Income Statement shown in Exhibit 7A on p.133 Spinning Wheels Bike Company. Scan vertically down the first column with its designated Value-Creating Domain categories. Notice how this new type of Income Statement collects all the financial results of the enterprise according to the sequential unfolding of value-creating activities.

Bargerstock's Income Statement creates four sections, one for each of the domains where it is easy to see the cost and profit impact in the sequencing of value-creating activities. Notice the four profit margin stages:

- **Sales and Marketing Activities Margin,** which reports both the realization of revenues and the cost of acquiring those revenues through marketing and selling activities
- **Factory Activities Margin,** which shows the next level of profit impact from the accumulation of costs related to producing goods and services for customers
- **Value Stream Margin,** which emerges after deductions for "traceable" back office support activities. Traceable activities are those back office operations that are directly associated with the specific value stream product families, that is, Street Bikes and Mountain Bikes. Anything that cannot be traced to one of the two Value Streams is treated as a common cost in the next section. Because Value Stream Margin activities are controllable by the Value Stream manager, this is the financial result that should be used for delivering performance-based compensation that is win/win/win.
- **Enterprise Income before interest and taxes** comes after deducting for common costs, which are not allocated across the two value streams because the costs are not controllable by the value stream managers.

Notice that both product families (Street Bikes and Mountain Bikes) spend about 10 percent of their value stream net revenues on sales and marketing activities. Normally, in a traditional Income Statement, selling and marketing expenses would be shown lower in an Operating Expenses section. But instead with this view showing Sales and Marketing Activities Margin, management's attention is continuously reminded about the effectiveness of the sales group as a value-creating work cell whose productivity can be measured similar to a profit center. Comparisons of these raw numbers and percentage breakdowns suddenly become easily accessible to Leadership. Time series data provide a powerful lens for evaluating the effectiveness of sales and marketing activities.

In the details on the Factory Operating Costs for SWB, it is apparent that there are better efficiencies in scrap and rework methods for Street Bike Group with costs reported as percentage of net sales revenue at 0.7 and 1.7 percent, respectively, compared to the Mountain Bike Group at

1.9 and 3.7 percent, respectively. In a lean-focused manufacturing organization, managers may want to track certain imperatives like scrap and rework as part of the changing priorities for business improvement. Accounting teams should be able to present internal financial statements as shown here to easily monitor progress on such initiatives.

To the Chart of Accounts, Add the Chart of Activities

When the Chart of Activities list is mapped and linked to the Chart of Accounts, then the Value Cycle Map can serve as one-page touchstone for reference by every associate as they think about the recipe for "what we do" and what can be done to improve the end-customer experience.

After the senior team documents its tacit value stream knowledge, it is a simple step to then link that behavioral framework directly to the financial framework by mapping the logic of the Income Statement as shown here and by building rigorous Key Performance Indicators that everyone involved can independently test and validate.

The Chart of Activities is a first element in building what Chuck Kremer in Managing by the Numbers calls "the Sacred Glossary." This Glossary is the "currently-in-use existing language" of decision making, which remains almost universally undefined (tacit) in US businesses of all sizes. See this book's glossary in the appendices.

A Chart of Activities within an integrated Value-Creating Activities Framework can connect operating activities directly to the bank account impacts they are generating—Cash Flow from Operating Activities. This connection creates a new reference point for stakeholders, investors, and bankers to evaluate the validity of the material assumptions underlying any cash flow projections they are given for loan consideration. Leaders recognize that this knowledge helps the enterprise prepare their case for loan applications.

With this understanding about how to create a dynamically alive Income Statement, you are now prepared for fast, fun, and flowing implementation of business reporting and execution. It is intended that this book provides a doorway to numbers that are alive, both activity-based and financial numbers that reveal the underlying reality effectively.

In the next chapter, we step back and review the full model of the Ballard Method and how it will serve you in building or rebuilding your enterprise to consistently high levels of performance, achievement and staff satisfaction.

Reference

IMA. (2006). *Accounting for the Lean Enterprise: Major Changes to the Accounting Paradigm*. Montvale, NJ: American Institute of Management Accountants.

CHAPTER 8

Boosting Enterprise Performance

Ballard's Alignment and Reporting Disciplines

1. *Map and Identify*: Map the sequence of VCAs; identify disconnects.
2. *Analyze and Project*: Three-bottom-line analysis with rolling cash flow projections.
3. *Define and Link*: Define financial drivers and disconnects; develop key KPIs linking activities and transactions.
4. *Engage and Align*: Engage leaders and staff by aligning on both true core facts and desired outcomes.
5. *Monitor and Report*: Regularly monitor performance in periodic huddles using outcome-driven agendas.

In this chapter, we assemble the full BARD method as the line of insightful inquiry that can create alignment of purpose across the entire enterprise, and unanimity about the priorities for improving value-creating activities.

In the introduction of this book, we described a long-standing puzzle called the "missing methodology." For decades, business experts and executives have sought to develop a systematic way to close the gap between business planning and business performance. Even today after so much that has been written about excellence in management, most organizations continue to fall short of accomplishing all their annual business objectives.

Now, **through Ballard's Alignment and Reporting Disciplines any enterprise can begin to close that performance gap**. Certainly, organizations that are struggling with performance can utilize BARD to get back on track. High-performing organizations can also benefit from BARD by learning how to harness the yet untapped tacit genius of their workforce . . . while transforming into a more dynamically collaborative workplace.

BARD is unique in its powerful ability to spark a line of inquiry leading to unanimity and ever-greater alignment of top management, leaders, and staff. The firm's value-creating activities alignment guides systematic flow, providing the framework for streamlining these activities. BARD awakens the tacit knowledge of employees by gradually pulling them into a dialogue of engagement that produces a host of benefits. Organizations who have used this methodology report the following among a wide variety of benefits:

- Higher profitability and operating cash flow
- Long-term customer delight and new prospect referrals
- More efficiently streamlined business processes
- A new or renewed advance in creating a learning, data-driven organization
- Higher job satisfaction and lower employee turnover

BARD is an exercise in leadership cultivated by the Reality Check first performed by the CEO, then shared with the CFO, and then with other senior managers. They form a Decision Team to build their unique value framework for steering toward excellence in delivering products and services to their customers, both internally and externally. By "modeling the way" on how to use the Value Cycle Map and assorted tools of **BARD**, the Decision Team gains credibility for its ability to train and lead.

The Reality Check creates an authentic experience of satisfying shared framework development that provides a solid foundation for knowing what is actually true and useful. Upon this platform of what is true and useful, the Decision Team is able to pull others into a nonthreatening line of inquiry about how the organization generates value for customers. Without such a systematic examination of the value-creating activities, organizations can get stuck in their old ways of doing things. They can become bureaucratic, rule-based machines where long-established policies and procedures supersede a nimble, awake awareness of the importance of adding value every day, responding to both internal and external customer expectations.

The Reality Check has templates that are available by request at www .businessexpertpress.com/books/mastering-leadership-alignment-linking -value-creation-cash-flow/, and consists of the first three of the five **BARD** disciplines listed below:

1. **Map Value Creation cycle.** In Chapter 2, we explained that instead of flowcharting the entire business system, which can become a labor-intensive project requiring weeks of refinements into the whole and involvement of a broad array of employees, targeted insights can be sufficiently gained by following these steps:

   a. **Develop a list** *sequencing* **value-creating activities,** across four domains:
      - Market Segmentation and Prospect Identification
      - Customer/Client Acquisition Sequence
      - Customer/Client Value Delivery Sequence
      - Back Office Support Activities
      - From this initially larger list, the CEO, the CFO, and the senior leaders will refine the list to somewhere between 19 to 21 most critical value-creating activity accounts.

   b. **Identify disconnects** in the core value-creating activities. Each participant will offer his or her own observation and tacit knowledge about the location of key breakdowns in the value streams. The accumulation of this information from an increasing circle of people provides food for rich discussions about priorities for improving the business.

   c. **Draft a Value Cycle Map (VCM).** This visual element is useful to promote an ever-evolving awareness of the importance of enterprise value-creating activities. Not only does it show the 19 to 21 core activity accounts, it eventually reveals the 3 to 5 most important measures and disconnects to be targeted as high priorities for improvement. The validated VCM is an important device for gaining and sustaining clarity of thought by all staff and thereby mature measurement momentum.

2. **Conduct three-bottom-line analysis.** In Chapter 3, we presented the guidance for senior leaders about how to continuously monitor the progress of the organization through three metrics:

   a. **Cash Flow from Operating Activities**. For sustainable business success, this number found on the Cash Flow Statement must be positive and growing. This amount is the real cash surplus generated by operations. It does not include investing (buying or selling of assets) or financing activities (issuance or retirement of debt or stock).

   b. **Net Profit**. This is the bottom line shown on the company's Income Statement using accrual accounting practices required of all publicly traded companies. It can vary significantly from Cash Flow from Operating Activities. The Income Statement presents a yardstick of enterprise profitability within a period. There is far less opportunity for the results to be engineered (manipulated) because revenues are realized when there is an arms-length transaction even if the cash is not collected. And, expenses are recognized when they are incurred even if they are not paid yet.

   c. **Return on Asset Stewardship.** This ratio of Net Income divided by Average Total Assets gives a return on investment calculation of how effective management is in its efforts to earn a profit on the total average assets employed during the year.

   All of these three bottom lines are critical touch points for managing any enterprise. It can be meaningful to compare your results to industry data to assess the health of the enterprise. Normally, we like to see organizations aspire to achieve upper-quartile results.

3. **Link financial drivers, disconnects, and key performance indicators (KPIs).** In Chapter 4, you saw how to create behavioral and financial scoreboard templates to effectively guide toward greater value creation excellence. The template includes 10 internal drivers and 2 external financial drivers.

   We provided a list of the 10 internal drivers of all financial results:

   - **Cash Driver** = Operating Cash Flow/Sales Revenue (a 'fuel gauge')
   - **Efficiency Driver** = Net Profit/Sales Revenue, often called Return on Sales
   - **Effectiveness Driver** = Sales Revenue/Average Assets, often called Asset Turnover

- **Three Expense Drivers**
  - Cost of Sales (or Goods Sold)/Sales Revenues
  - Marketing, Selling, General and Admin Expenses/Sales Revenue
  - Salaries Expense/Sales Revenue in service and distribution companies

    OR
  - Research and Development Expenses/Sales Revenue
- **Three Turnovers** related to Receivables, Payables, and Inventory Days
- **Fixed Asset Driver** = Net Profit/Average Net Fixed Assets

In addition to these 10 internal drivers, we presented two external drivers that address the perspectives of creditors and stockholders:

- **Banker's Driver:** Total Debt/Assets Ratio
- **Investor's Driver, a.k.a., Return on Equity:** Net Income/ Average Common Stock Equity

If senior managers diligently monitor these metrics, they are more likely be able to diagnose changing trends and identify problems early. And in Chapter 4, we started with a method to identify KPIs that can guide your organization's efforts toward improving value for customers. The measures coming from this inquiry are the same ones that will be periodically updated in three to five KPI loops on the Value Cycle Map.

4. **Engage/Align leaders, then staff.** In Chapter 5, you discovered the subtle secrets of engaging senior managers that ultimately can lead to a cascading effect throughout. Through alignment of the brain of the CEO to the value-creating activities of the organization and the subsequent alignment of other senior managers, the foundation gets built to invite others into the adventure of building whole-hearted unanimity.

5. **Monitor and report performance.** In Chapter 6, we discussed the ways to institutionalize and sustain enthusiasm for your efforts to create a highly engaged, problem-solving, value-streamlining enterprise that emerges by tapping the tacit knowledge of the senior team. We revealed tips and suggestions for conducting effective huddle meetings every 2 to 4 weeks to sustain energy and attention on the core tasks for improving business processes.

Through these five Ballard Agility and Reporting Disciplines, you have the model for transforming into a high-performing enterprise, a leader in your industry.

Key Reminders about BARD Implementation:

- **Allow data to lead the way.** The big idea here is that by continuously building a solid foundation of whole-hearted unanimity on the core set of basic enterprise facts, first doing a thorough test with the senior team, before attempting broader engagement, staff alignment will grow incrementally as enterprise agility grows abundantly.

- **Maintain consistently the rule about not sharing documents with anyone until they complete their own topic-specific Reality Check.** Avoid attempted collaboration until each person has completed the exercise of articulating his or her own tacit knowledge of value creation in writing (or notes taken). It is often counterproductive to engage someone in a dialogue about improving value-creating activities unless he or she has deliberated and/or thought about value streams. In Ballard's case experience, much if not most conflict at work comes from attempting to collaborate meaningfully before either the leadership and staff have fully debriefed themselves and each other about what are the true facts, or developed their considered insights regarding those facts.

- **Activity precedes transaction in all cases.** To understand financial results, we need to understand how human behavior generates those results. W. Edwards Deming stated the vast majority of business problems are associated with improperly designed business processes. If there is poor performance, it is usually not because people do not want to do well. Instead, their performance is restricted by a poorly designed process (Deming, 2013). The work of BARD tackles this problem head-on by systematically defining the sequence of value-creating activities and then identifying the breakdowns and pinpointing where they originate and affect subsequent activities. In this way, we gently re-align business processes and the behavior that is forthcoming from those processes so that there is minimum waste and maximum value to stakeholders. For requesting self-assessment templates, which are helpful for applying Value Creation and Alignment concepts to any enterprise, as well short white papers illustrating approaches to improving performance measurement from a variety of sizes and types of enterprises, see www.MOSupgrade.com/MLA /Library

Case Study Summaries

Three client summaries show the impact of BARD methodologies. For more case details, refer to the Appendices.

Case #1

Oklahoma Blood Institute

Overview

As the second-largest blood manufacturer in the United States, in 2007 Oklahoma Blood Institute (OBI) employed 700 people along with 800 volunteers, while producing $68 million in annual revenues.

After a decade of steady growth, with some earlier scaling challenges, OBI's leadership could see industry challenges ahead. Having been tasked with spearheading a metrics-driven culture change, CFO Randy Stark decided to use Ballard's Management Operating System Upgrade™, still in use in 2016.

Business Problems

- Flattening of revenue growth
- Lower than desired capabilities in problem definition and creative problem solving
- Need for improved cash flow and margins

Management Operating System Upgrade Tools Utilized

- CEO and CFO Reality Checks
- Financial Scoreboard

- Chart of Activities
- KPI Integration Launch
- Management Scoreboard Executive Briefing
- Decision Team and KPI Impact Measurement Teams
- Monthly All-Hands Huddles

Unexpected Windfall

While working to improve one of the KPIs, a team found a heretofore hidden source of significant cash waste. CEO Dr. John Armitage estimated that "The savings over the next 12 months from just this side discovery? At least $150,000 to $250,000."

Business Results at OBI

- Cash reserves doubled from under $4 million to over $8 million in 18 months
- Doubled profit from 3.5 to 7 percent in 18 months
- Cash Flow from Operating Activities increased over $12.4 million in the first 60 months, averaging >100% improvement every year for those 5 years over the year before the MOS Upgrade.
- Senior staff reported that Dilbert-type hallway conversations evaporated in less than 90 days, replacing by discussions on value creation, disconnect mitigation, and KPI development.
- The Institute went from whom to be acquired by to whom to acquire by the end of year 1, and an acquisition was completed in less than 2 years.

Key Person Quotes:

When the board heard reports of the more than doubling of both profit from under 3.5% to over 7%, and cash reserves from under $4 million to over $8 million within 18 months after the huddles launched, I knew that our organization development initiatives had come together. Our lean manufacturing, change initiatives, strategic planning and leadership development had combined well with the *methods, tools and practices to upgrade our Management Operating System (MOS).* **Andrew Gin, MD, Former Executive Committee of the Board of Directors**

In combination, (BARD has produced) a good shift in OBI's culture, and a success on the financial front. We are more metrics-driven and cost containment conscious. Many initiatives have been positively impacted by the huddles. We also have wider appreciation for our overall position vis-à-vis industry pressures. (BARD) makes it more meaningful as it is a dedicated forum to weave the external realities into the discussions of tangible internal issues. **John Armitage, MD, CEO**

I think we are the best managed we have ever been in the history of OBI. We are really changing the whole culture, by changing the way we look at how we measure and operate as an organization. **Mark Patterson, VP of Finance and Development**

Case #2

NAPA Auto Parts Distributor, Northern California

Overview

The NAPA Auto Parts distribution franchise in Santa Rosa, California, used BARD as a core engagement and participation mechanism for generating self-managing leadership—creating a leadership team with applied business acumen that turned around the declining trends of the business unit to produce new growth in margins and operating cash flow.

This 70-year-old NAPA franchise suffered from dramatic swings in profitability and operating cash flow. Rarely had it achieved two consecutive profitable quarters. After successfully engaging the Five Disciplines, NAPA improved inventory accuracy, boosted operating cash flow, and produced 13 consecutive quarters of profitability.

The key factor in the change was engaging a team of nonfinancial leaders and associates to become co-architects of the financial outcomes in collaboration with the CFO and the CEO. Since the initial MOS Upgrade in 2006, the monthly Performance Management Group "huddles" had been sustained with no further outside support. After 4 years of monthly huddles, CEO Rick Call decided to huddle twice a month, because he has found it so critical to "keeping everyone's eye on the ball."

Business Problems

In late 2005, after a decade and a half of steady contraction resulting in reduction of workforce from more than 100 people to less than 70, the pressure from national chain competition had not abated. The franchise had been experiencing continuous swings of profit and cash flow, and leadership never knew what profit or operating cash flow was going to be until the period closed and finance provided the monthly statements. Among the business problems that needed attention were the following:

- Profit peaks and valleys; smoothing desired
- Poor inventory control and count accuracy
- Excessive low-profit inventory; low levels of high-profit inventory
- Long accounts receivable aging period
- Inconsistent cash flow hindered financing approvals
- Customers reported dissatisfaction with handling of overdue accounts.

Management Operating System Upgrade Tools Utilized

- CEO and CFO Reality Checks
- Financial Scoreboard
- Chart of Activities
- KPI Integration Launch
- Management Scoreboard Executive Briefing
- Decision Team and KPI Impact Measurement Teams
- Monthly All-Hands Huddles

Results

- Thirteen consecutive quarters of profitability after years of profits and losses
- Dramatically improved inventory accuracy and reduced SKU count

- Improvement in cash flow from operating activities averaged over a half a million dollars per year for the first 5 years of the upgrade.
- 22 percent reduction in average age of accounts receivable
- Improved customer interaction and better pricing leading to more clients
- Improved ability to forecast financials and obtain additional working capital financing
- Improvements led to growth through competitor acquisition

Key Person Quotes:

It just blew me away that (our team) was grasping that we can set our own course here! **Ken Thengval, CFO**

After trying to solve every issue at once, we finally had clarity on which one to focus on first to get the most impact, and then where to go next, once that one is resolved. **Franchise Purchasing Manager**

Now that we were beginning to benchmark the key indicators, I was confident we could create the multiples that Jahn said we could expect, and I was understandably gratified they actually occurred so much faster than we expected. **Ken Thengval, CFO**

Case #3

Indigenous Designs

Overview

This case shows how full application of BARD allowed an apparel company to sustain profitability in spite of competitive market pressures. This summary reveals how and why the CEO, President, and Finance Director valued the MOS Upgrade rollout.

Background

Pioneering cofounders, Scott Leonard (CEO) and Matt Reynolds (President), along with a dedicated team have been building a leading fair-trade organic clothing company in the United States for decades. This founding B Corporation has built a network of suppliers in the Andes that over time has been composed of nearly 1,000 weavers, stitchers, and knitters who are being paid fair-trade wages. Many of the Indigenous contractors are women working from their homes as they create top-quality clothes for the after-action sportswear and organic fabric fashion markets in North America.

Building on this unique supply chain foundation, Indigenous had been responding to increased market pressures beginning in 2008. Cost control, inventory management, and improved financial performance became imperative. In 2009, a new finance director (Jennifer Clark) was hired to help support that effort.

Business Problems

- Inconsistent profits after a decade of building extensive supply chain infrastructure
- Absence of a regular forum for collaboration on company-wide problems
- Need to improve the staff's financial-operational acumen, including understanding financial statements, and especially understanding the connections between cash flow (financial acumen) and staff activities (operational acumen)

Management Operating System Upgrade Tools Utilized

- CEO and CFO Reality Checks
- Financial Scoreboard
- Chart of Activities
- KPI Integration Launch
- Management Scoreboard Executive Briefing
- Decision Team and KPI Impact Measurement Teams
- Monthly All-Hands Huddles

Results

The company systematically improved its effectiveness in transforming business strategy into operational excellence. Among the many benefits that were realized from the BARD intervention, Indigenous reported the following:

- Generated 6 years of profitability following previous 10 years of planned losses to build supply chain
- Significantly improved cash flow
- Reduced excess inventories
- Increased focus on a few KPIs to drive business results
- Improved staff engagement, understanding, and morale
- Enhanced customer retention
- Development of a regular forum for problem identification and problem solving
- Improved communication across functional roles

Key Person Quotes:

We spent over a decade building a sustainable and equitable supply chain to the standards of our vision for fair-trade commerce. When I looked closely at upgrading our Management Operating System, I knew it would help us, as it was now the time for everyone to understand how we are financing what we have built, and measuring financial performance so that we can improve it. I believe it was Lord Kelvin that said, "To measure is to know. If you cannot measure it, you cannot improve it." - **Scott Leonard, CEO and Co-Founder**

And then, hours into this meeting - I wish I had a camera—the entire room just lit up—I could see it—that all of a sudden, everyone understood why they had gone through all these financial and operational diagnostic exercises together. - **Jenn Clark, Finance Director**

This will help us bring our day-to-day disciplines to driving the big picture numbers and hitting the 5-year big benchmarks we have to hit in the long term. There is great power in bringing this structure, framing and philosophy to our longer-term vision. - **Matt Reynolds, President**

Typical BARD Improvements

These mini-cases summarize typical patterns of business improvement through BARD methods:

- Enhanced capabilities for meeting and exceeding customer expectations
- Improved cash flow from operating activities
- Improved profitability
- Enhanced employee morale
- High levels of employee satisfaction and engagement
- Significantly elevated creative data-driven problem-solving capabilities

Effectiveness of the Ballard Method (BARD)

When properly implemented, the Ballard Method generates outstanding improvements in organizational outcomes because of the following characteristics of its approach:

1. **The Ballard Method wakes up the organization to its purpose to create value for customers.** To begin the journey toward unanimity and alignment within an enterprise, everyone's awareness needs to become fully awake and aware to the purpose of creating high-quality, value-added products and/or services. Engagement of customers through focus groups establishes a direct link to acquire feedback about how well the organization is meeting or exceeding customer expectations.

2. **The Ballard Method is based on natural laws of organizing through the principle of flow.** Both humans and businesses are open systems that exchange matter and energy with their environments. Open systems theory describes how natural systems evolve through continuous internal reorganization to minimize the resistance to flows of matter and energy.

   The heart and core of BARD is transparent lean management, which is a natural-law-based approach that cultivates flow. Flow is promoted by understanding the value-creating activities so that non-value-added activities can be eliminated, resulting in more streamlined and highly efficient business processes.

3. **The Ballard Method is rigorous yet straightforward.** The method is data driven and behaviorally based. Priorities for improvement projects come from participants' observations of breakdowns in the value-creating activities. KPI impact measurement teams pursue data collection for measuring and benchmarking improvement activities.

   By tapping the inherent (tactic) knowledge of leaders and staff who possess intimate knowledge of how business processes work and break down, the path to improvements becomes well defined and improvement alternatives are explored. It is understood that staff behaviors and activities will change when the underlying enterprise design and value creation measurement approach supports their capabilities to achieve excellence. The method requires discipline and responsibility to follow through on commitments.

4. **The Ballard Method generates feedback loops to sustain progress.** Many management initiatives fail because of waning attention on priorities. Employees get consumed with "fighting fires" on a daily basis. Their attention gets diverted to the urgencies of the day. The intermediate or long-term priorities previously established get shelved. Through the Ballard and Kremer's Huddle magic, we have a way of regularly meeting and reporting on improvement projects. This keeps the Decision Teams focused and responsible for continuous attention on improving results. The ultimate feedback loop comes through improvement in Cash from Operating Activities, which is a key litmus test of authentic business process improvement.

Jeff Lueken, CEO, Lueken's Food Stores, Reflects on Use of KPIs through BARD

Re-centering the business on cash flow and the understanding of this key bottom line is critical. OCF, being the only tangible bottom line, is now a lens by which all people's activities are viewed.

Kudos for the glossary: outlining the meaning of key KPIs and making the case for their importance is an index of GREAT enterprise info along with the Chart of Activities accounts. Many of these are easy to understand intellectually, but to get their full meaning and weight, one has to track, and then "experience" them. BARD demonstrates that observing the impact to these measures drives operating activity changes. Newfound clarity creates a sense of urgency to address the right key leverage points. (After well over a year of senior team preparation, 30 self-selecting leaders and staff launched their MOS Upgrade in a 6 hour KPI Integration Session in the fall of 2016. Search youtube for Joe Lueken of Lueken's Village Foods on ABC's Good Morning America for the story of this exemplary family-founded and now employee-owned local food institution)

Leadership and the Missing Methodology Discovery

The Ballard Method provides the behavioral tools to engage others in the adventure to achieve whole-hearted unanimity by inspiring a shared vision, by modeling the way, by challenging business processes, by enabling others to act, and by encouraging the heart of associates (Kouzes and Posner, 2012). As such, the Ballard Method fulfills the criteria for the Missing Methodology described in the introduction of this book. More precisely, the Method lays out systematic, step-by-step procedures for (a) understanding the enterprise value-creating activity sequence, (b) discovering the obstacles to the flow of value, (c) revealing the connections between activities and transactions, and (d) regularly monitoring progress to continuously and collaboratively re-sharpening focus for business improvement.

Now, with the palette of Ballard Method tools examined in this book, you are better prepared when you use them, to lead toward higher achievements that benefit customers, stockholders, other stakeholders and your personal quality of work life. Keep us informed on your challenges and successes with BARD, if you please.

References

Deming, W.E., and Orsini, J. (2013). *The Essential Deming: Leadership Principles from the Father of Quality*. New York, NY: McGraw-Hill.

Kouzes, J., and Posner, B. (2012). *The Leadership Challenge: How to Make Extraordinary Things Happen in Organizations*. 5th edition. San Francisco, CA: Jossey-Bass.

Exhibits

Exhibit 2A

Cascading of BARD Implementation

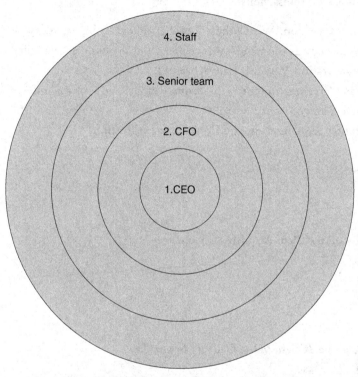

1. & 2. Establish core of unanimity with senior leader and the scorekeeper (CFO)
3. Valid foundation established with whole-hearted senior team unanimity in place to mine staff tacit job knowledge

Exhibit 2B

Value-Creating Activities Sequence Template

Principle: Activity precedes transaction in all cases, leading and creating all financial transactions.

Focus Question: What is the sequence of value-creating activities we follow to generate a satisfied and loyal customer, and all our financial results?

Organization Mission (One Sentence):

Value-Creating Activities in Sequences: Fill in as many numbers as needed for your work system.

Market Segmentation and Prospect Identification

1)

2)

3)

Etc.

Customer/Client Acquisition Sequence

1)

2)

3)

Etc.

Customer/Client Value Delivery Sequence

1)

2)

3)

Etc.

Back Office

1)

2)

3)

Etc.

Generated by _____ on [DATE] _____.

Access this template at www.MOSupgrade.com/MLA/Library

Exhibit 2C

MACPA Value-Creating Activities Sequence

Focus Question: What is the sequence of value-creating activities we follow to create thrilled and delighted customer?

Organization Mission: Helping CPAs achieve success.

Market Segments and Prospect Identification

1. Engage potential members in the following ways:
   - Promote student memberships (high school and college)
   - Promote candidate memberships (post-college, pre-CPA certification)
   - TCPA website
   - 100 percent membership program with firms
2. Swearing-in ceremony with Maryland Board of Public Accountancy

Membership Acquisition and Value Chain

3. Town halls
4. Seminars/conferences/summit
5. Customized training
6. Legislative advocacy and grassroots organizing
7. On-line communities
8. Peer-review program
9. Endorsed products and services—affinity
10. Second life training
11. Blogs
12. List servers
13. Podcasts
14. Newsletters
15. E-mails
16. Issue alerts on emergency issues

Back Office:

17. Annual billing i
18. Member profile update online and with dues notices
19. Follow-up in fall months for unpaid dues

Generated CoA originally on 9/13/10 between JW Ballard and Skip Falatco with numbered content © all rights reserved to MACPA 2010

Exhibit 2D

MACPA Chart of Activities Draft with Disconnects (Partial View)

Membership Acquisition Sequence	Disconnects (Breakdowns)
1. Engage potential members in the following ways:	
1a. Market to CPA nonmembers	* Limited information about newly licensed CPAs
1b. Promote student and candidate memberships	* Next generation is more group resistant
1c. 100 percent membership program with firms	* Firms are not looking to spend more money
1d. Swearing-in ceremony with MD State Board of PA	* Challenging to engage newly minted CPAs
2. Deliver WOW customer service at every opportunity	* Time consuming and need a fully committed staff
3. Continue to engage and inform existing members in the following ways:	* Getting the information members need; Engaging members to receive the value available to them
3a. Seminars/conferences/summit/chapters	* CPE competition coupled with larger firms doing their own training
3b. Customized on-site training	* Scalability of delivering customized training
3c. Town halls	* Getting more than 20 percent of members to attend
3d. On-line communities	* Having difficulty finding viable product
3e. Legislative and regulatory advocacy and grassroots	* CPA resistance to politics
4. New products and services	* Can be challenging to inform members of products
5. Second life training	* Members sometimes have difficulty with technology
6. Podcasts	* Great content—more people should utilize
7. Newsletters	* Some states moving away from newsletters. Mature product?
8. E-mails	* Competing with a flood of e-mail
9. Communicate with members to educate and inspire	* Members are busy. It is a challenge to engage them

Exhibit 2E

MACPA Value Cycle Map

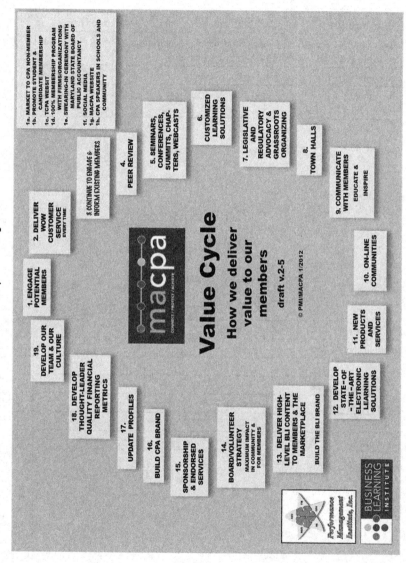

Exhibit 3A

3 Bottom Lines

Bottom Line	Calculation	Meaning
Cash flow from operating activities aka OCF	Cash generated and expended from value-creating activities	Sustainable value creation
Net profit	Sales revenue - expenses	Surplus over costs
Return on Asset (stewardship)	Net income/Average assets	Asset utilization and effectiveness

Exhibit 3B

ZYY Corp

Income Statement
2015

Sales revenues	$1,225,000	100.0%
Cost of goods sold	(530,000)	43.3%
Gross profit	695,000	56.7%
Operating expenses	(542,050)	44.2%
Income before taxes	152,950	12.5%
Income taxes	(30,000)	2.5%
Net income	$122,950	10.0%

Exhibit 3C

ZYY Corp

Balance Sheet
12/31/15

Assets		Liabilities	
Current Assets:		**Current Liabilities:**	
Cash	$ 142,800	Accounts payable	$ 53,000
Receivables	35,000		
Inventory	62,000	**Long-term Liabilities:**	
Prepayments	12,000	Notes payable	540,000
Total current assets	$ 161,800	**Total Liabilities**	$ 593,000
Long-term Assets:		Owner's Equity	
Buildings & Equip (net)	860,000	Common stock	$ 100,000
		Retained earnings	418,800
		Total Owner's Equity	518,800
Total Assets	$1,111,800	**Total Liab. & Owner's Equity**	$1,111,800

Exhibit 3D

ZYY Corp

Cash Flow Statement—Indirect Method (GAAP)
2015

Cash Flow from Operating Activities:

Net income	$122,950	
Adjustments to reconcile:		
Depreciation expense	5,000	
Increase in accounts receivable	(300)	
Increase in inventories	(40,000)	
Increase in prepaid expenses	(2,350)	
Increase in accounts payable	38,000	
Decrease in accrued expenses	1,000	
Net cash received from operating activities		$ 124,300

Cash Flow from Investing Activities:

Cash paid to purchase equipment	$(101,000)	
Net cash used for investing activities		$(101,000)

Cash Flow from Financing Activities:

Cash from new short-term debt	$ 58,500	
Cash paid for dividends	(9,000)	
Net cash received from financing activities		$ 49,500

Change in cash during 2015	$ 72,800
Beginning cash balance (1/1/15)	$ 70,000
Ending cash balance (12/31/15)	$142,800

Exhibit 3E

ZYY Corp

Cash Flow Statement—Direct Method 2015

Cash Flow from Operating Activities:

Cash received from customers	$ 150,300	
Cash paid for inventory purchase	(14,000)	
Cash paid for employee compensation	(8,000)	
Cash paid for office overhead and supplies	(2,000)	
Cash paid for interest expense	(500)	
Cash paid for various taxes	(1,500)	
Net cash received from operating activities		$ 124,300

Cash Flow from Investing Activities:

Cash paid to purchase equipment	$(101,000)	
Net cash used for investing activities		$(101,000)

Cash Flow from Financing Activities:

Cash from new short-term debt	$ 58,500	
Cash paid for dividends	(9,000)	
Net cash used for financing activities	$ 49,500	

Change in cash during 2015		$ 72,800
Beginning cash balance (1/1/15)		$ 70,000
Ending cash balance (12/31/15)		$142,800

Exhibit 3F

Financial Scoreboard MACPA Example

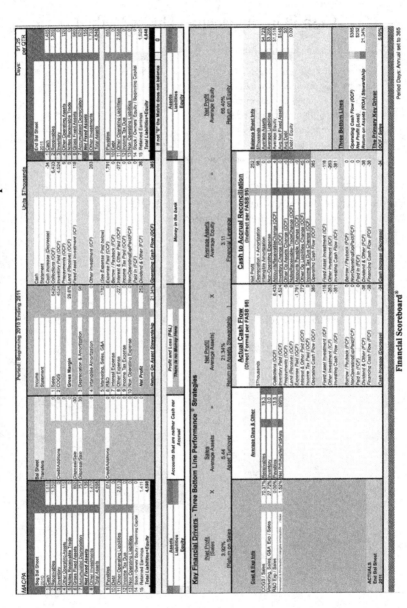

Financial Scoreboard®

Access this template at www.MOSupgrade.com/MLA/Library

Exhibit 3G

Financial Scoreboard Accounts Mapping Template

Balance Sheet FSB Field	Cash Flow	Code	Balance Sheet ACCOUNT(s) NAME	Income (P&L) Statement FSB FIELD	Cash Flow	Code	Income Stmt ACCOUNT(s) NAME
Cash		1.	Cash				
Accounts Receivable	O	2.	Receivable	Sales	O	1.	Total Support & Revenues
Inventory	O	3.		COG/COS	O	2.	Expenses
Other Operating Assets (short term, non-depreciable, eg. Prepaids)	O	4.	Prepaid Expenses				
Notes Receivable Trade¹	O	5.					
Gross Fixed Assets (gross property, plant & equipment)	I	6.	Fixed Assets				
(Accumulated Depreciation) of fixed assets	I	7.	Accumulated Depreciation	Depreciation & Amortization	I	3.	
Net Fixed Assets	I		Net Fixed Assets				
Other Investments (eg. Goodwill)	I	8.	Other Assets	Intangible Amortization (eg. Goodwill amortization)	I	4.	
Total Assets			Total Assets				
				Marketing, Sales, G&A	O	5.	Supportive Services
Accounts Payable	O	9.	Accounts Payable	R&D	O	6.	
Debt (long term >1yr)	F	10.	Total Current Liabilities	Interest Expense (FSB version 2.02 and earlier include this in Other Expense cell)	O	7.	
Other Operating Liabilities (short term, eg. Untaken earned vacation)	O	11.	Accrued Expenses	Other Expense (income)	O	8.	
Income Tax Due	O	12.		Income Tax Expense	O	9.	
Non Operating Liabilities¹	F	13.	Long Term Liabilities	Non Operating Expense¹	F	10.	
Stock / Owners' Equity / Beginning Capital	F	14.					
Retained Earnings (+ Net Income if periods are Quarterly or Monthly)	F	15.	Retained Earnings	Net Profit			Changes in Net Assets
Total Liabilities & Equity							

Cash Flow Affected: O = Operating, I = Investing, F = Financing   ¹ Often zero, but Check with CPA.   (x) watch sign

Access this template at www.MOSupgrade.com/MLA/Library

Exhibit 3H

Return on Asset Stewardship Graph by Asset Turnover and Return on Sales

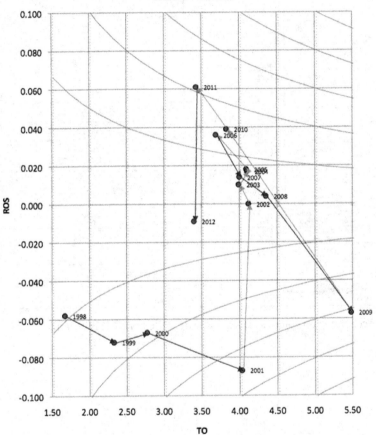

**MACPA ROA
1998–2012**

Access this template at www.MOSupgrade.com/MLA/Library

Exhibit 4A

"Tachometer" 15-Year Reading/Key Drivers/Pro Forma MACPA History 1998–20011 and 2012 Projected

Dollar Trend

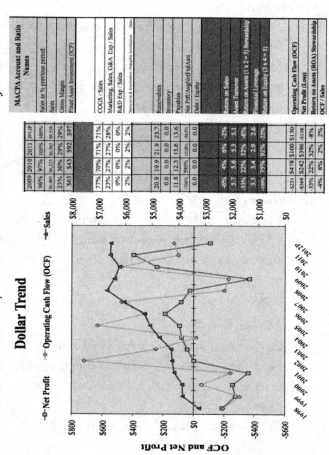

	2009	2010	2011	2012P	MACPA Account and Ratio Names
					Sales as % previous period:
	96%	97%	105%	100%	Sales
	$6,485	$6,223	$6,562	$6,536	
	23%	30%	29%	29%	Gross Margin
	$65	$43	$92	$97	Fixed Asset Investment (ICF)
	77%	70%	71%	71%	COGS / Sales
	23%	27%	27%	28%	Marketing, Sales, G&A Exp / Sales
	0%	0%	0%	0%	R&D Exp / Sales
	2%	2%	2%	2%	Depreciation & Amortization–Tangible & Intangible, Straightline Amortization ... Sales
	20.9	19.9	21.9	23.7	Receivables
	0.0	0.0	0.0	0.0	Inventory
	11.8	12.3	13.6	13.6	Payables
	-796%	599%	1218%	-367%	Net Pft/AvgNetFxdAss
	0.0	0.0	0.0	0.0	Debt / Equity
	-6%	4%	6%	-2%	**Return on Sales**
	5.7	5.6	3.3	3.1	Asset Turnover
	-33%	22%	32%	-8%	Return on Assets (1 x 2 = 3) Stewardship
	3.3	3.4	2.9	2.6	Financial Leverage
	-109%	75%	92%	-22%	Return on Equity (3 x 4 = 5)
	-$231	$478	$100	$130	Operating Cash Flow (OCF)
	-$368	$242	$396	-$108	Net Profit (Loss)
	-33%	22%	32%	-8%	Return on Assets (ROA) Stewardship
	-4%	8%	2%	2%	OCF / Sales

Exhibit 4B

Material Assumptions Index
MACPA FY2012 Projections

A. Income/Profit and Loss:

Revenue Plan

- 2.5 percent annual growth in total revenues with assumed linear changes breakdown
- decrease in seminar revenue of 4.5 percent
- growth in conference revenue of 6 percent
- flat computer course revenue
- growth in in-house revenue of 10 percent
- growth in facilitation revenue of 167 percent

Operating Cash Flow: goal of positive operating cash flow

Key Drivers:

- 4 percent annual growth in COGS (direct CPE expenses)
- 4.5 percent decline in marketing, sales, general, and admin. expenses due in part assumed loss of one full-time equivalent position
- Goal of 40 percent gross margin on CPE revenue

Balance Sheet:

- Receivables—assumed to follow trend of recent years
- Fixed assets—assumed to follow recent asset purchases
- Investments—assumed to grow at a rate similar to the previous 2 years
- Debt—assumed that debt will not be added

Access this template at www.MOSupgrade.com/MLA/Library

Exhibit 5A

MACPA Chart of Activities and Disconnects

Membership Acquisition Sequence	Disconnects (Breakdowns)
1. Engage potential members in the following ways:	
1a. Market to CPA nonmembers	* Limited information about newly licensed CPAs
1b. Promote student and candidate memberships	* Next generation is more group resistant
1c. 100 percent membership program with firms	* Firms are not looking to spend more money
1d. Swearing-in ceremony with MD State Board of PA	* Challenging to engage newly minted CPAs
2. Deliver WOW customer service at every opportunity	* Time consuming and need a fully committed staff
3. Continue to engage and inform existing members in the following ways:	* Getting the information members need; Engaging members to receive the value available to them
3a. Seminars/conferences/summit/ chapters	* CPE competition coupled with larger firms doing their own training
3b. Customized on-site training	* Scalability of delivering customized training
3c. Town halls	* Getting more than 20 percent of members to attend
3d. On-line communities	* Having difficulty finding viable product
3e. Legislative and regulatory advocacy and grassroots	* CPA resistance to politics
4. New products and services	* Can be challenging to inform members of products
5. Second life training	* Members sometimes have difficulty with technology
6. Podcasts	* Great content—more people should utilize
7. Newsletters	* Some states moving away from newsletters. Mature product?
8. E-mails	* Competing with a flood of e-mail
9. Communicate with members to educate and inspire	* Members are busy. It's a challenge to engage them

Exhibit 6A

Improvement Tracking Report: Key Disconnects and KPIs
Data Mining Company

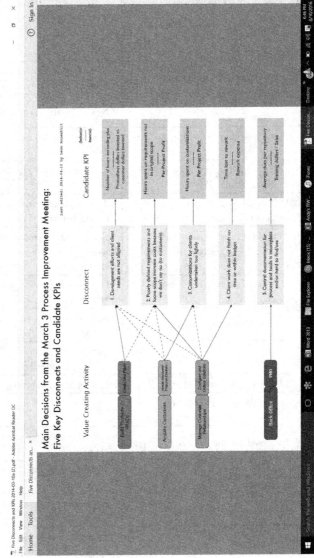

Exhibit 6B

MACPA "Tachometer" and "Fuel Gauge" 1998–2011 Actuals

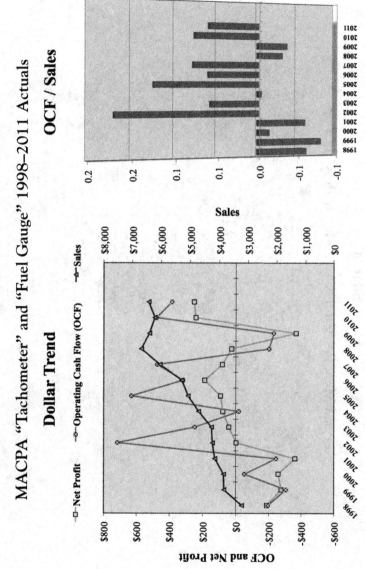

Exhibit 6C

Revised MACPA Value Cycle Map with KPI Loops

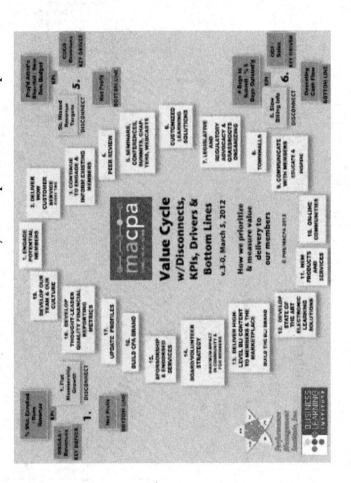

Exhibit 7A

Chart of Activities: Four Domains	
Market Segment/Prospect ID:	MP
Customer Acquisition:	CA
Customer Delivery System:	CD
Back Office Support:	BO

Spinning Wheel Bikes Value Stream Income Statement 2015

		Product Family Value Streams					
		Combined	%	Street Bikes	%	Mountain Bikes	%
Domain							
	Marketing & Selling Activities:						
CA	Gross Sales Revenue	$ 20,854,000	114.3%	$ 13,100,000	113.7%	$ 7,754,000	115.4%
CA	Less: Returns & allowances	$ (1,013,000)	−5.6%	$ (800,000)	−6.9%	$ (213,000)	−3.2%
CA	Less: Sales Discounts	$ (1,600,000)	−8.8%	$ (780,000)	−6.8%	$ (820,000)	−12.2%
	Net Sales Revenue	$ 18,241,000	100.0%	$ 11,520,000	100.0%	$ 6,721,000	100.0%
CA	Selling Activities	$ (1,130,000)	−6.2%	$ (720,000)	−6.3%	$ (410,000)	−6.1%
MP	Marketing Activities	$ (688,000)	−3.8%	$ (408,000)	−3.5%	$ (280,000)	−4.2%
	Total Selling and Marketing Activities	$ (1,818,000)	−10.0%	$ (1,128,000)	−9.8%	$ (690,000)	−10.3%
	Sales & Marketing Activities Margin	$ 16,423,000	90.0%	$ 10,392,000	90.2%	$ 6,031,000	89.7%
	Factory Activities:						
CD	Materials purchased	$ (6,460,000)	−35.4%	$ (4,200,000)	−36.5%	$ (2,260,000)	−33.6%
CD	Labor Incurred	$ (1,935,000)	−10.6%	$ (1,135,000)	−9.9%	$ (800,000)	−11.9%
CD	Fixed and Variable Overhead Incurred	$ (805,000)	−4.4%	$ (500,000)	−4.3%	$ (305,000)	−4.5%

(Continued)

Exhibit 7A (continued)

Domain		Product Family Value Streams					
		Combined	%	Street Bikes	%	Mountain Bikes	%
	Marketing & Selling Activities:						
CD	Scrap Costs	$ (210,000)	-1.2%	$ (80,000)	-0.7%	$ (130,000)	-1.9%
CD	Rework costs	$ (450,000)	-2.5%	$ (200,000)	-1.7%	$ (250,000)	-3.7%
	Total Factory Activities	$ (9,860,000)	-54.1%	$ (6,115,000)	-53.1%	$ (3,745,000)	-55.7%
	Factory Activities Margin	$ 6,563,000	36.0%	$ 4,277,000	37.1%	$ 2,286,000	34.0%
	Traceable Value Stream Back Office Activities:						
BO	General Activities	$ (415,000)	-2.3%	$ (230,000)	-2.0%	$ (185,000)	-2.8%
BO	Administrative Activities	$ (485,000)	-2.7%	$ (270,000)	-2.3%	$ (215,000)	-3.2%
BO	Warranty Cost Activities	$ (360,000)	-2.0%	$ (200,000)	-1.7%	$ (160,000)	-2.4%
	Traceable Back Office Activities	$ (775,000)	-6.9%	$ (430,000)	-6.1%	$ (345,000)	-8.3%
	Value Stream Margin	$ 5,788,000	29.1%	$ 3,847,000	31.1%	$ 1,941,000	25.7%
	Common Back Office Costs:						
BO	Executive Compensation	($1,560,000)	-8.6%				
BO	HQ office expenses	($630,000)	-3.5%				
BO	General liability insurance	($170,000)	-0.9%				
	Total Common Costs	($2,360,000)	-12.9%				
	Adjustment to GAAP Absorption Costing	$610,000	3.3%				
	Enterprise Income before interest and taxes	$4,038,000	19.5%				
	NOTE: % Change in Inventories:			Street		Mtn	
	Raw Materials			7.2%		1.4%	
	Finished Goods			-3.2%		-6.8%	

Exhibit 7B

Spinning Wheel Bikes Breakdown of Selling Expenses 2015

	Street	%	Mountain	%	Total
Sales Prospecting - base	$ 190,000	26%	$ 118,000	29%	$ 308,000
Sales Lead Generation	$ 54,000	8%	$ 32,000	8%	$ 86,000
Sales closing (commissions)	$ 283,000	39%	$ 146,000	36%	$ 429,000
Sales Travel costs	$ 93,000	13%	$ 50,000	12%	$ 143,000
Sales Support salaries	$ 47,000	7%	$ 28,000	7%	$ 75,000
Sales Support supplies	$ 25,000	3%	$ 18,000	4%	$ 43,000
Sales Phone, internet, etc.	$ 28,000	4%	$ 18,000	4%	$ 46,000
Totals	$720,000	100%	$410,000	100%	$1,130,000

Executing on the Theory of Constraints

The Theory of Constraints says that in any complex work system, the value throughput of that work system is governed by a single primary bottleneck, or constraint, and that the primary constraint is most often both invisible and counter-intuitive.

The constraints are usually invisible governors. The whole system can only function as well as its worst constraint(s), what Jack Stack, pioneering author of classic *Great Game of Business,* calls the key vulnerabilities, or what is sometimes called the weakest link in the chain. Those constraints can only be found through a systematic process of discovery—applying the scientific method to test and validate any assumptions about what are the greatest constraints, or what could be called system disconnects. The question is how to find those few dynamic constraints, vulnerabilities, or disconnects, such that when they are improved, the whole system's value throughput will automatically be improved across the board.

The first formal Operations Research project provides a good way to illustrate that there is always one primary constraint in any work system. The story is about a refinery in Texas in the 1960s. The company did a study measuring the mathematics of the fluid flow dynamics in the entire facility. They then described mathematically how those fluid flows were connected to the economic results created by the total refinery operations. Operations Research was a new discipline that used science to build what was called an objective function model. In those days, refineries had very large pipes in the center for the larger fluid flows, and then successively smaller and smaller pipes out toward the periphery for the secondary, tertiary, and other minor fluid flows. A seemingly reasonable design.

When they built an objective function model of the whole process, the math showed them that the little tiny pipes way on the periphery were actually slowing down the fluid flows in the largest pipes, and in fact functioned as a governor on the total fluid throughput potential, and the financial performance, of the entire facility. Since that time all refineries have been built with the same size pipes throughout. That situation was invisible, so they could not realize that was happening until they had laid out the mathematical blueprint of how all the fluid flowing in all the piping actually worked when tied to all the financial transactions. Thank you to Bill Veltrop for sharing his project story.

In the case of NAPA Auto Parts Management Operating System Up-grade™, the primary constraint turned out to be consistent inaccuracies in the inventory counts. They had known that was an issue for many years, but until we all thought it through together, with help from the Three-Bottom-Lines perspective and a blueprint of all the activities, it was not obvious that it was in fact the one crucial problem to focus on first. The results, once they picked that focus, were a surprise to everyone, espe-cially how fast and how much everything improved, as that one constraint may have been costing as much as all the others combined.

Nine No-fee Value Creation Self-Assessment Templates

Enabling readers to implement sample work products shown in the MLA exhibits applied to any enterprise—available upon request at www.MOSupgrade.com/MLA/Library.

A) **Chart of Activities Brainstorm #1 (MACPA Case - Exhibit 2B):**
Brainstorm, select, and sequence value-creating activities in four domains: Market Segmentation & Prospect ID, Customer Acquisition, Value Delivery, and Back Office

B) **Kremer/Hood Performance Measures Assessment (Indigenous Case - Exhibit 2):**
A one-page tool showing overall financials with Three Bottom Lines, Key Financial Drivers, and operational performance indicators currently tracked and/or projected

C) **Financial Scoreboard (FSB) Accounts Worksheet (Exhibit 3G):**
For use with the FSB, map summary Balance Sheets and Income Statement (P&L) relevant line items to FSB Financial Statement format to guide accurate entry in the FSB.

D) **Demo - Financial Scoreboard (FSB) (Exhibit 3F): Password is FSBv0**
Perform a one-period reconciliation to see three bottom lines, 12 key drivers, the financial matrix as a whole, and three different versions of Cash Statements. FSB Accounts Worksheet and full SOHO case numbers from *Managing by the Numbers.*

E) **Ballard Material Assumptions Index (MACPA Case - Exhibit 4B):**
A simple tool for recording material assumptions underlying financial projections (pro formas). Makes it easy to document all assumptions for any account, actual or future.

F) **Value Stream Income Statement Template (Exhibit 7A):**
An Income Statement breakdown by product families, organized around Ballard's Four Value Creating Activities Domains with layers of profit margin revealed.

G) **RoX Plotter (Return on X)—courtesy of Walt Niehoff (Exhibit 3D and IBM Case).**
Copy excel sheet with IBM Financial Performance data from 1950 to 2008—Enter the same data for any enterprise on the copy to see Mobley's ROA Chart for that data.

H) **Highest Priority Benefits of an MOS Upgrade™ (1 page)**

Identify the most important current priorities in your enterprise that would be served/resolved by a Management Operating System Upgrade™

I) **ROA Graph Pencil Worksheet**

Plot your ROA Graph by hand with this simple worksheet.

Additional Value Creation Self-Assessment Templates available at www.MOSupgrade.com/MLA/Library

J) **Financial Scoreboards (FSB) with five, thirteen or sixteen periods – FSBs 1, 2, or 3**

Three Bottom Line Performance unifies all transaction events from the summary financial statements (P&L/Income Statement, Balance Sheet, Cash Flow Statement) into one simple framework that enables ever more accurate projections of future cash flow.

K) **Value and Cash Leaks Matrix:**

Assess Management Operating System performance in six dimensions on a scale from Basic to World Class: Goal Sharing, Financial Literacy, Operational (non-financial) Indicators, Financial Indicators, Problem Seeing and Problem Solving, Cross-training.

L) **Chart of Activities (CoA) Worksheet**

The Chart of (Operational) Activities is a complement to the Chart of (Financial) Accounts. This worksheet is a place for one to record and update with new information: the Account on the Chart of Activities, CoA notes, Disconnect Account Names, Disconnect notes, and Key Driver Linkages.

M) **KPI Matrix**

A set of spreadsheets for working on and presenting as a whole the Chart of Activities, Disconnects in the Value Cycle, and Key Performance Indicators that measure the Disconnects.

N) **CEO/COO Enterprise Performance Management Assessment**

A high level, whole system, performance management assessment from the 'Captain of the Ship's point-of-view.

O) **Organization Trust Assessment - courtesy of Dr. Dean Spitzer and AMACOM:**

Self-assess levels of organizational trust—searching questions to score—Benchmarks provided.

Case Synopsis

Oklahoma Blood Institute

"I think we are the best managed we have ever been in the (45 year) history of OBI. We are really changing the whole culture, by changing the way we look at how we measure and operate as an organization." OBI VP of Finance & Development, Mark Patterson. The Oklahoma Blood Institute (OBI) has over 700 employees, almost $90 million in revenues, 800 volunteers, and thousands of blood donors, producing up to and over 150,000 blood units/year. OBI manufactures the highest-quality blood products in the United States, and is the nation's second largest blood manufacturer.

After a decade of steady growth to $68 million in 2007, with some earlier scaling challenges, OBI's leadership could see that the issues in the industry as a whole were catching up with them. Randy Stark, CFO, having been tasked with spearheading a "Metrics-driven Culture Change," decided to use the Management Operating System (MOS) Upgrade™ to meet the challenge. The total cumulative impact of the OBI Management Operating System upgrade for the first 5 years was a net gain of over $12.4 million of new operating cash.

Results

Former Member of OBI's Executive Committee of the Board, Dr. Andrew Gin, M.D., says: "When the board heard reports of the more than doubling of both profit from under 3.5 to over 7 percent, and cash reserves from under $4 million to over $8 million within 18 months after the huddles launched, I knew that our organization development initiatives had come together. Our lean manufacturing, change initiatives, strategic planning and leadership development had combined well with the methods, tools and practices to upgrade our Management Operating System (MOS). Particularly valuable were the hands-on skill-building and highly effective monthly meeting structures, whose one-page agenda method has been copied throughout the organization."

Every year for the next 5 years, as financial improvement teams continued to integrate multiple improvement initiatives, they delivered a better than 100 percent average improvement in annual cash flow from operating activities (OCF), compared to the their OCF the year before upgrading their MOS. Cash results were more than doubled each year, over the year prior to upgrade, for 5 years in succession.

Early in the second quarter, three huddles into OBI's Management Operating System Upgrade, CEO John Armitage, M.D., said, "We have gone from zero to sixty in a very short time, and the engagement levels are outstanding."

Examples of Impacts from the Management Operating System Upgrade

In OBI's second monthly Performance Management Team all-hands Huddle, an unsought but critical idea bubbled up. They found a hidden source of significant cash waste.

A manager in another team was studying her personal, laminated, 8x11 OBI Value Cycle Map. It prompted her to ask the right questions about a standard operating procedure not accomplishing anything. It created no value-add for any external or internal customers and had been taking needed resources for over a decade. Within a few minutes of discussion, all the pieces fell into place. They green-lighted the new policy 10 days later. CEO Dr. John Armitage estimated: "The savings over the next 12 months from just this side discovery? At least $150,000 to $250,000. This is a good example of fulfilling the promise for why we are implementing (an MOS Upgrade)."

The specific results that they saw because of this unexpected new insight added to the multiple crucial improvements that were already starting to cohere by focusing on small core of master measures. As the MOS Upgrade continued, the learning environment more completely and continuously transferred measurement leadership capability to each team member.

One core MOS Upgrade element creates an explicitly shared language in the form of a glossary for value creation in the enterprise. Everyone now had the same understanding—"This is everything that we do here, this is what we call it and this is the sequence in which we do it." They learned to track and leverage what was most important in driving enterprise value, by creating and validating an integrated set of Key Performance Indicators (KPIs) and Key Leading Indicators. The MOS Upgrade trained and habituated OBI's people to craft, validate, and present the master and secondary metrics they chose, which measured first their activities, and then linked them to the financial results their combined activities continuously generated.

The MOS Upgrade formed cross-functional teams of key OBI staff, which continue almost 10 years later, to be responsible for driving operational changes to improve financial results. Each KPI Impact Team focuses on one of the master measures created by the group as a whole, in ongoing iterations. Using one-page agenda templates, those team members have a meeting pattern totaling only two-and-a-half hours per month of each person's time, or less. Over the years, the primary focus of each team has continued to be developing, updating and presenting one-page KPI status reports called "Activity Statements," showing the master measures at the regular all-hands huddles, confirming how they connect to transactions, then assessing and driving improvement.

The KPI Impact Measurement Teams focus primarily on a few master measures of everyone's value-creating activities. They look at "Three-Bottom-Line" financials; in the context of a small set of Activity Statements: one-page dashboards of validated master measures of operating activities (as opposed to financial transactions), with both past and future trending. These "behaviorals" (which complement and drive the "financials") are developed and reported by their staff. By measuring themselves, means is provided for OBI to connect the operating activities to the financial transaction results. OBI now has the visibility over its own enterprise to choose which operating activities to increase or decrease in order to optimize its financial results.

"In combination, there has been a good shift in OBI's culture, and a success on the financial front. We are more metrics-driven and cost containment conscious. Many initiatives have been positively impacted by the huddles. We also have a wider appreciation for our overall position vis-à-vis industry pressures. Huddles make it more meaningful as they are a dedicated forum to weave external realities into the discussions of tangible internal issues". John Armitage, M.D., CEO.

Case Study

Indigenous Designs

Overview

This case shows how the Management Operating System (MOS) Upgrade™ with Ballard's Five Disciplines helped enable organic apparel company Indigenous Designs to establish and sustain profitability in spite of competitive market pressures. The case reveals how the CEO, President, and Finance Director all valued the roll-out and results of Ballard's Five Disciplines in uniquely different ways.

Cofounder and President Matt Reynolds reports, "The MOS Upgrade helped button up our operations. It provided us with methods and tools to define a value creation framework that was more adaptable because it was new to everybody at once, even as the content itself was very familiar. Engaging and aligning leaders, then staff (**Discipline #4**) requires behavioral changes towards collaboration by allowing data and creativity to lead the way."

"For the executive team, this process has added value by bringing more focus within different departments that the executive team oversees, and provides a lot more structure for measuring against specific tasks that we are tackling. The process strongly encourages the team to jointly pick a few select KPI-related tasks (Key Performance Indicators), working only on these tasks until problems are solved and KPI's are validated or completed. An important element to the success of this program was setting up a foundation of trust and patience early on. This foundation has empowered the team to be creative long-term and not focus merely on short-term solutions."

"It was millions of dollars in value to us over the 5 years we've applied these tools and practices so far. Absolutely." Scott Leonard, Cofounder and CEO

Background

Pioneering co-founders, CEO Scott Leonard and President Matt Reynolds, along with a dedicated team, have been building a leading fair-trade organic clothing company in the United States since 1994. This Founding

B-Corporation (which certifies their commitment to sustainability) has built a network of suppliers in the Andes that over time has comprised 1500 weavers, stitchers, and knitters, who are being paid "fair-trade" wages. Many independent contractors are women who work a small business from their homes as they create top-quality clothes for the after-action sportswear and organic fabric fashion markets in North America.

Building on this unique supply chain foundation, Indigenous had been responding to increased market pressures beginning in 2008. Cost control, inventory management, and improved financial performance became imperative. In 2009, a new finance director, Jennifer Clark, was hired to help support that effort. She helped further professionalize the finance function and inventory controls.

The management team identified the following key business issues that needed immediate attention:

- Inconsistent profits after a decade of investing heavily in supply chain infrastructure
- Absence of a regular forum for collaboration on company-wide problems
- Need to improve the staff's financial-operational acumen, including understanding financial statements, and especially understanding the connections between cash flow (financial acumen) and staff activities (operating activities acumen)

The Intervention: A Management Operating System Upgrade™

In 2010, Jahn Ballard was engaged to implement an upgrade to Indigenous' MOS—the tools and practices by which the company runs itself—by hands-on training of leaders and staff to collaborate in new ways. They learned how to measure what matters (growing what Dean Spitzer in *Transforming Performance Measurement* calls "measurement maturity"[1]), and to make routine their use of the newly upgraded tools and practices. After using the Financial Scoreboard to provide participants a simple overview of the financial side for their monthly meetings (**Discipline**

---

[1] See *Transforming Performance Measurement*, AMACOM Books, 2007.

#2), the whole staff collaborated to develop a visual representation—a map—of their "Value Cycle" (**Discipline #1**), showing the sequence of value-creating activities from market definition, to product design and marketing through production, sales, and post-sale customer service.

In two eight-hour problem-solving and rapid-prototyping sessions, also known as a *Kaizen* events in Lean Manufacturing terms, staff surfaced and were able to clearly see the key disconnects throughout the company that were impeding its value-creating activities. Then we asked them the question, "What are the most relevant behavioral and financial data points that will give us a way to measure either how bad this disconnect really is, or how well we are improving the situation described by this disconnect?," which resulted in more than a dozen *candidate* Key Performance Indicators.[2] Finally, they selected the three to five candidate KPIs that the whole company agreed provided *the most opportunity for enhancing overall company performance* (**Discipline #3**).

CEO Scott Leonard expressed his perspective about how the Five Disciplines met Indigenous' strategic and operational needs: "I believe it was Lord Kelvin who said, 'To measure is to know. If you cannot measure it, you cannot improve it'. We spent over a decade building a sustainable and equitable supply chain to the standards of our vision for fair-trade commerce. When I looked closely at the MOS Upgrade approach, I knew it would help us, as it was now time for everyone to understand how we are financing what we have built, and measuring financial performance so that we can improve it."

Upgrading the MOS in 2011 turned out to be both profitable and positive in terms of Operating Cash Flow. During 6 straight years of modest profitability, through consistent monthly huddles and one-page reporting refinement by the KPI Teams installed during the Upgrade, the whole organization sustained a significant and consistent pattern of improvement. Indigenous Designs **Exhibit 1** on p.152 shows a graph of the actual financials from 2009 and 2010, with projections through 2015. It was used in a pitch deck to investors for Indigenous "Series B" capital raise. The Financial Scoreboard permitted indigenous to easily develop

---

[2] A "candidate" KPI is one that the team hypothesizes is a strong measure of value creation, and then tests to see if it *truly* is a strong measure.

much more accurate and more useful projections, displayed simply in an unbroken continuum with past, actual financial results, so that everyone at all levels can easily understand the past and present results connect with intended results for the future.

The MOS Upgrade uses a Financial Scoreboard to view not just one bottom line, but all Three Bottom Lines: (1) Operating Cash Flow on the Cash Statement, which shows *how much cash the company has had, or will have*, under current material assumptions; (2) The classic Bottom Line of profit or loss on the Income Statement, which shows the status of company contracts; and (3) Return on Asset, the Bottom Line derived from the Balance Sheet, which shows how the status of company *property* has been stewarded, linked to the Income Statement as Net Profit.

With FSB, there are no longer three separate financial statements, but rather a completed puzzle that solves the problem of understanding how the financial statements all work together as a whole; and how to use the financial statements as tools to manage the business. The FSB both bridges to all the statements with Three Bottom Lines, and reveals the complete set of 12 key financial drivers that mathematically create all three of the bottom-line results.[3] These drivers constitute all the possible drivers of transaction results. Only a few of the 12 will be operative in any given enterprise. Therefore, it is very powerful when everyone knows which ones to focus on (and correspondingly which ones to stop wasting effort on).

An MOS Upgrade structures KPIs to include an operational data point paired with a financial data point so that changes in operational performance can connect directly to, and so reveal, impact(s) on financial transactions. The Financial Scoreboard reveals those changes in financial performance by focusing on which of the 12 Key Financial Drivers are most affected by a particular KPI. The FSB was instrumental to figuring out which of these key drivers were operative in Indigenous' business because, with correctly designed and validated KPIs in place, it reflects how changes in operating performance drive financial performance.

---

[3] As identified by Louis Mobley at IBM in the 1960s, who later drove the adoption of FASB reg. 95 in 1987 (FASB is the Financial Accounting Standards Board).

Upgrading the MOS helped Indigenous identify *which of the key drivers* are their business's most important by creating KPIs and testing them for being the *right KPIs* for running their particular enterprise.

As Scott shared, "There comes a time in the evolution of a CEO when one recognizes the importance of being truly in sync, and flowing with what is happening in the Income Statement, Balance Sheet and Cash Flow statement all at once." It is no mean feat to achieve that level of understanding and flow. At Indigenous, Scott had led a number of good attempts before using a Three-Bottom-Line approach with the Financial Scoreboard, but each turned out to be either too simplistic or too complicated to be both useful and sustainable as ongoing practices. The MOS Upgrade's measurement self-auditing disciplines and Financial Scoreboard made it easy for Scott to finally get there. It gave him the clarity and confidence in understanding the complex interplay of his business's operational and financial activities to hand over the actual internal project management for upgrading the Management Operating System to his Finance Director.

Indigenous Designs Exhibit 2 on p.153 shows the benchmark created, against which any subsequent changes in performance were to be recorded, including Indigenous Three Bottom Lines, Key financial drivers, and Key nonfinancial numbers. To assess and benchmark an enterprise's performance measures, see KH Performance Measures template at www.businessexpertpress.com/books/mastering-leadership-alignment-linking-value-creation-cash-flow.

Reflecting on the KPI Integration and Management/Accounting Unification one-day *Kaizen* events in **Discipline #2**, Scott felt that "One of the key lessons that came to me was the power of being silent while my people worked on issues normally confined to the Executive Team. My commitment to supporting the learning, rapid-prototyping and financial projecting process was to be present, but to 'not talk' during the deep dive into the financials through Three-Bottom-Line analysis with the entire team. It was surprisingly valuable to allow my whole team to struggle and tussle with what financial statements really were all about."

"Although it was personally almost painful to not come to their aid at times, it was profound to see them make their way through it together in the *Kaizen*, without my direct assistance. We had done a tremendous amount of work as a whole to optimize our margins, and it was great the way the simple pictures and color-coding helped everyone to see more clearly what we had all already accomplished with expenses and inventory efficiencies, especially."

"In the KPI Integration *Kaizen* the disconnect process was so powerful because it allowed employees to engage and take ownership. Clarifying and validating the material they had submitted previously, was then applied both to value-creating activities and driving the development of the candidate system KPIs."

Jennifer Clark, Finance Director—MOS Upgrade Internal Project Manager

"The first two days of the kick-off of the MOS Upgrade were grueling until everyone finally got it. I wish I had a camera—the entire room just lit up—I could see that all of a sudden, everyone understood why they had gone through all these operational, and then financial diagnostic exercises together."

"For me, that made my job so much easier, even if we had never gone forward from that moment—because the whole company now knew how all the pieces fit together. Everyone could see their place within the work system. It has driven such an excitement. We have moved from 'You have to come to these meetings'—to they can't wait to have their huddles because they are making a difference. Now, employees see how they are making a difference—and how they can continually improve their capacities as both individuals and as key performance teams."

Indigenous Designs Exhibit 3 on p.154 shows a KPI Matrix® documenting "the Value Creation Accounting" framework draft from the initial KPI *Kaizen*. The exhibit documents all the learning the company as a whole did during the *Kaizen*. As the team looked at this situation, they realized among other things that they needed to track the possibility that some inventory may be too old. The KPI was developed called "Carrying cost/aging," which means that inventory is tagged by its age category and an estimate of carrying costs, such as warehousing, labor, and overhead. This encouraged liquidation of inventories as they aged.

During the KPI *Kaizen*, teams were formed to gather more data and refine the KPIs so they would be more and more useful as tools for continuous improvement, as a regular feature of how Indigenous would now "run itself," using its upgraded Management Operating System.

Matt Reynolds, President and Cofounder, continues, "People want to make decisions fast. We are in a business situation where decisions and deadlines are hitting every day. The MOS Upgrade approach creates a distinction between the rush of events, and stepping back to solve the big problems. This is a big-picture project that takes the approach of steering the large ship, versus every day short-term deadlines on the deck. Now, we are putting together a long-term strategy for solving key issues such as retention rates, inventory turns, and return rates in order for the ship to reach its final destination. By bringing the whole company in on this process, I really do believe it is transformative."

"I also appreciate the subtle element of accountability involved with the new group meeting structure that did not take place when meetings were isolated like in the past. There is tremendous energy and account-ability one feels when standing in front of the entire company and saying, 'I am going to do this'. It brings the employee back to the reason for being a part of the team—The process re-focuses the team, everyone wants to succeed. So, it brings it back to 'I've got to make that call—I've got to get back to that project and make it happen, because I said it in front of everybody.' This was really powerful, and the most effective way to create constructive change, by unifying everybody. **A large part of this pro-gram's success was how the upgrade was initiated. It was introduced in a patient, positive, and encouraging way."**

Results

Through consistent monitoring and reporting (**Discipline #5**), Indigenous systematically improved its effectiveness in transforming business strategy into operational excellence. Among the many benefits that they realized from the MOS Upgrade, Indigenous Designs reported that they had:

- "Millions of dollars" of savings and new margin (per Scott Leonard, CEO)
- Created 6 years of profitability following prior 10 years of planned losses

- Reduced excess inventories
- Increased focus on a few KPIs to drive business results
- Improved staff engagement, understanding, and morale
- Enhanced customer retention
- Implemented a regular forum for problem identification and problem solving
- Improved communication across functional roles
- Established common language for key business terms, eliminating inefficiencies arising from miscommunication

Summary and Conclusions

The Indigenous Designs case provides an executive-level view of how company culture and activities are transformed through an MOS Upgrade. At Indigenous, the company had been scaling its operations to solidify its supply chain, but had not yet achieved profitability. As a result of implementing new inventory controls, and their MOS Upgrade, they became not just profitable, but sustainably profitable. The executives at Indigenous felt that Ballard's five Alignment and Reporting Disciplines, with the related tools and practices, more than proved their value, providing a more collaborative and effective path toward sustained profitability and improved operating cash.

Indigenous Designs Exhibit 1

Trend of Profit, Sales, and OCF—2 Years Actual, 5 Pro Forma

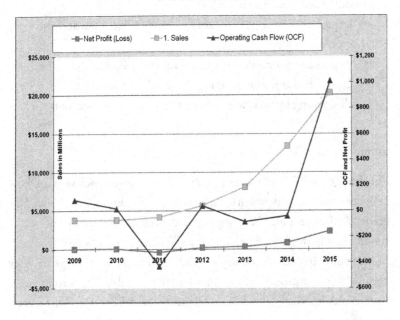

Indigenous Designs Exhibit 2

Kremer/Hood Performance Measures Assessment

Image from MOS Upgrade Financial Scoreboard and Activity Data. This shows in the lower right the nonfinancial measures of activities that drive the financial results. The left side is where one would see Indigenous Designs' Three Bottom Lines (actual numbers removed for confidentiality) and which of the 12 Key Drivers are present in their business model. Access this template at www.businessexpertpress.com/books/mastering -leadership-alignment-linking-value-creation-cash-flow.

PMI KREMER/HOOD PERFORMANCE MEASURES ASSESSMENT

Indigenous Designs
(Company Name)

2009   T = Tracked
(Year)   P = Projected

Three Bottom Line Performance
Define overall measures

Key Financial Drivers &
Define specific measures

Key Operating Numbers *
Define behavioral measures

T		P		T			P
x	Operating Cash Flow (OCF)		Weekly Cash Balance	Fixed Asset Investment x	Capital Budget Planning		x
				↓ Receivable Days x			x
	Assets			↓ Inventory Days x	Dead and Returned		x
	Liabilities			↑ Payable Days			x
x	Net Profit	x	I year	↓ COGS/Sales x			x
x	Sales	x		↓ MSGA/Sales x			x
x	Expenses	x		↑ Sales/Net Fixed Assets			
	Return on Sales (ROS) Net Profit/Sales times (x)				% of Over production of Inventory - set goals x		
	Asset Turnover (AT) Sales/Total Assets				Transportation costs per unit x		x
	equals (=)				Expenses per Marketing Activity - x		x
	Return on Assets (ROA) Net Profit/ Total Assets				Working on Design, Samples, Prototypes indicators		
					Capacity - understanding of vendors		
	OCF/SALES						

DuPont Formula

* Any critical number that gives a metric for focusing on workflow, and how that flow of work relates to both the customer (ext'l. or int'l.) and overall financial results. Can be a bottom line, key driver, sub-driver, or key performance indicator.

PDT: "People Doing Things"   © 2003-2004 Ballard/Kremer/Hood

This material is from the Financial Scoreboard and Managing by the Numbers by Kremer, Rizzuto, and Case.   Visit www.financialdashboard.com

Indigenous Designs Exhibit 3
Partial Picture of KPI Matrix®

This partial depiction of Indigenous KPI Matrix shows how the Matrix uses color and words to distinguish between a Chart of Activities (operational activities performed in the value creation cycle labeled Value Chain in this case) in yellow, linked to system Disconnects in the value creation cycle in blue, with master measures (3-5 "system level" priority KPIs, the most important measures of value creation system wide) in green, and key measures (next-level KPIs that support continuous improvement) in black. Indigenous Designs updated this 2010 Matrix in 2014, which led to a second branding and sales breakthrough, very different from the ones that occurred in the 2010 *MOS Upgrade sessions.*

Indigenous fair trade + organic — **Agile Accounting & Management - KPI Matrix**

	Value Chain	Disconnects	Key Performance Indicator (KPI)	Votes
1	Development & Demographic Sign-off	a. Design refinement data missing - Retailer sell thru		
2	Design Products	a. Unknown cost to develop / carry each SKU	2a. Ranked Sales by SKU	1
			2a. Catalog Real Estate Performance	
3	Procure Development (Dev) Samples			
4	Merchandizing, Cut & Finalize Line			
5	1st Line Revision	a. **Specs are wrong**	5a. Returns / Sales for Branded	3
6	Procure Sales Samples			
7	Merchandizing - Brand Strategy	a. End Consumer awareness is low		
8	Create Marketing Collateral		8a. Proactive Leads / Total Marketing $	
9	Samples & Collateral to Sales Rep force			
10	Attend Trade Shows & Mail Out Collateral	a. Time required for booth set up & tear down	10a. Trade Show Costs (all in) / Sales $ Generated	
			21a. Labor Costs / Time Required	3
11	Final Line Revisions			
12	Sell to Customers - Inside Sales & External Sales Reps	a. **Customer productivity unknown**	12a. Branded sales / total customers	5
			12a. Support $ / number of customers	
13	Obtain Customer Orders	a. Style editing not occurring		
		b. **Manual reporting - sales tracking and forecasting**	21a. Labor Costs / Time Required	3
14	Approve Terms, Credit Check & Set Up New Customers	a. Setting up new Accounts		
15	Issue PO's to Vendors		15a. Consolidation thresholds	2
			15a. Production Minimums	2

Notice the sequential flow of the three columns from left to right as the team implemented. **Discipline #2**—Value Chain mapping and identification of disconnects; **Discipline #3**—Development of system KPIs as master measures for guiding people with their progress on improvements, and driving transactions with unanimous priorities.

Case Synopsis

IBM Mobley ROA (Return-on-Asset Stewardsip) Chart 1950 to 2008

IBM's executives used the one-page chart in IBM Case Exhibit 3 on p.159 to guide IBM's Net Profit and Asset growth between the years of 1957 and 1978.

The upper left corner of Exhibit 1 on p.146 is 1950, the starting place where Lou Mobley (mob-lee) first began serving as a coordinator of hiring thousands of engineers. Lou helped set up the Sand's Point Executive School curriculum for Tom Watson, Jr. in 1955. He spoke often at events that CEO Watson could not attend, throughout the greater DC to Boston corridor. Being a stand-in for Mr. Watson continued until Lou's retirement in 1970. The frequency of speaking slowed way down after Lou was sent by Watson to turn around the Federal Systems Division in Maryland, where he retired after turning the division around.

Prior to these assignments, in 1952 he led the marketing team that coined the term "data processing". In 1953 and 1954, Lou managed the committee that built IBM's world-renowned internal training curricula as well as cultural norms transmission and learning systems.

Lou invented the ROA Chart in Exhibit 1 as a tool to argue with DuPont's Treasurer (who is why the name Du Pont as in the DuPont Formula) in 1952, that showing only a single percentage numbers for ROI (seen here on the right hand scale) was virtually meaningless in and of itself, as there are an infinite number of points where that same number can be place anywhere on the curve. Lou gave up trying to convince DuPont and the market in 1956, deciding instead to simply implement his ROA Chart as an executive leadership and performance improvement tool, supporting divisional profit-planning disciplines initiated throughout IBM in 1957. This DuPont ROA Chart version (IBM Case Exhibit 1) was created by Walt Niehoff using IBM's Graphpak Software in 2001.

The Mobley DuPont ROA chart shows clearly that the single ROA percentage could be an infinite number of points along those curved, dotted lines. Where a point falls, and therefore its meaning, depends on whether the business unit is stronger at controlling costs (Efficiency), in which higher Return on Sales shows in the upper left, or at converting capital and assets into improved market share (Effectiveness) by moving Asset Turnover results to the right.

The Mobley DuPont ROA Chart guided and tracked budget development, helping to more than double IBM's Return on Asset Stewardship from around 18 percent in 1957 to over 42 percent in 1978. This means that in 1978, while being one of the largest and fastest-growing companies in history, IBM returned a profit of nearly half (42+ percent) its total asset value in that 1 year!

The Mobley DuPont ROA Chart version in IBM Case Exhibit 2 on p.160 was created by Walt Niehoff using Excel® in 2013. Labels for the vertical and horizontal scales changed over time, as evinced by different labels from the 1950s to today. Chuck Kremer chose Return on Sales for the vertical, and recommended Asset Turnover as the best label for the horizontal.

The Mobley DuPont ROA Chart in IBM Case Exhibit 3 on p.161 is a one-page handout from an internal IBM Management program. Here you can see the DuPont Equations of IBM's ROA trajectory during the 20 years that Lou Mobley served the company, training the CEOs, Senior Executive, and many managers in personal and organizational leadership development. Under the title Divisional Profit Planning, IBM's leadership used this chart to help guide the development of what was called a "balanced plan."

Every year IBM's next year's profit planning had an embedded critical success factor: creating financial results where the increase of efficiency (short term/profit margin focus) by raising Return on Sales was balanced by a similar increase in Asset (Capital) Turnover, thereby balancing cost control with increased sales effectiveness (long-term/market share focus). This means that one ideal period-to-period progression of results should move on a trajectory of increasing ROI perpendicular to the dotted curves throughout the trajectory.

Notice that it took them until 1962 to figure out how to tune the entire company to achieve that ideal trajectory and then recover some more balance to the past margin improvements the next year by having higher effectiveness improvement than efficiency. Control Data Corp. entered the service bureau business in 1964, so they retooled the whole company with a perfectly balanced two-year internal investment strategy, which they market-tested with great effectiveness in 1967. That perfectly teed IBM up for a huge leap to almost 37 percent ROA in 1968.

IBM Case Exhibit 4 on p.162 shows US Industrial Return on Investment using Mobley ROA Chart for the years 1962 to 1966, (but were changed to '01-'04 for CPA Professional Education purposes). At Sand's Point, Mobley used this ROA Comparison Chart above to train IBM Sales executives to understand the US Economy. When the US Industrial Averages were compiled and reported as a national aggregated United States Economy Balance Sheet and Income Statement, the data showed several different kinds of patterns of business performance, which combined to the average for 4 years in the 1960s, shown circled. The upper right and lower left ROA patterns show the two primary business models of the time. Companies in the lower right tended to be newer companies that invested heavily in growth, and are now being forced to pay attention to margins at the cost of market share. Companies in the upper left are highly focused on maintaining margins, but weak on turning over the assets at a higher rate to achieve higher market penetration.

He suggested that when doing pro forma projections, that the intent should be an ideal of increasing all three bottom lines incrementally— growing Profit, Operating Cash Flow, and Return in synergy with each other. He asserted that the ideal way to increase Return on Asset Stewardship was to make incremental and ideally similar scale changes (small and steady improvements) in both Return on Sales (Efficiency) and Asset Turnover (Effectiveness). So when testing projections for their bottom-line impacts, it is ideal to have relatively equal improvements in both efficiency and effectiveness that are steady over time, rather than herculean pushes to improve only one or the other.

Lou emphasized another thing to bear in mind, which is that improving effectiveness (Asset Turnover) is generally the far harder of the two. His encouragement was that if losses in either dimension are unavoidable then plan for that explicitly, as IBM did from 64 to 66 (IBM Exhibit 3 on p.161), and then plan your turnaround as they did in 67 and 68, and attempted to do, but lost ground on effectiveness in 1969.

Walt Neihoff has made all of us a gift of an open-source ROA charting tool, the ROA Chart that you have seen (IBM Case Exhibit 2) showing IBM ROA from 1950 to 2008. If you would like to create a chart like this to track your own return numbers history, and drive its future, go to the book's site, and request the tools folder. It is available as a simple Excel® template at www.MOSupgrade.com/MLA/Library (IBM Case Exhibit 5 is a paper chart blank that can be used to chart enterprise ROA with a number 2 pencil or pen).

Alfred Sloan, working with Donaldson Brown, originally implemented the math (named the DuPont Equations in 1952) for tracking internal efficiency and effectiveness improvement at General Motors in the late 1920s, because Sloan realized that was the only way he could get accurate enough internal feedback to be able to beat Henry Ford to make GM the largest automobile manufacturer in history; which took him decades.

Any leadership and stakeholder team that can connect what they do every day with vision and intention focused on sustained and balanced, simultaneous improvement of effectiveness and efficiency will inevitably be a dominant player in any market it chooses to serve; by aligning objective facts with the team's highest service aspirations.

DISCLAMER: The materials in this ROA sample case came from JW Ballard's direct interactions and co-teaching with Lou Mobley from 1980 to 1987. Walt Niehoff has made the priceless contribution of a thoroughly referenced and footnoted paper on how to use the math to visualize the "DuPont Formula" for Return on Investment. This case by Walt Niehoff on Lou Mobley and IBM is to be considered the definitive source on ROA charting, and can be found in the tools and white papers folder that can be requested at www.MOSupgrade.com/MLA/Library

IBM Case Study Exhibits

IBM Mobley ROA (Return-on-Asset Stewardship) Chart

IBM Exhibit 1

Return on Investment (Return on Asset Stewardship) from 1950 to 2000

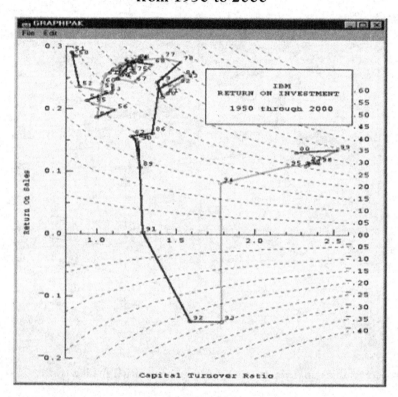

IBM Exhibit 2

Return on Investment (Return on Asset Stewardship) from 1950 to 2008

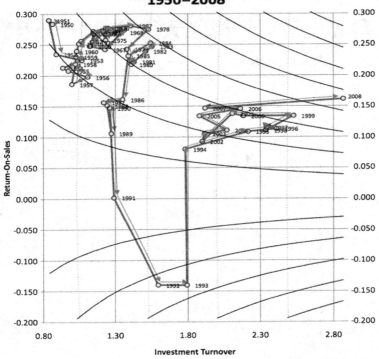

Access this template at www.MOSupgrade.com/MLA/Library

IBM Exhibit 3

Return on Investment (Return on Asset Stewardship) from 1950 to 1970

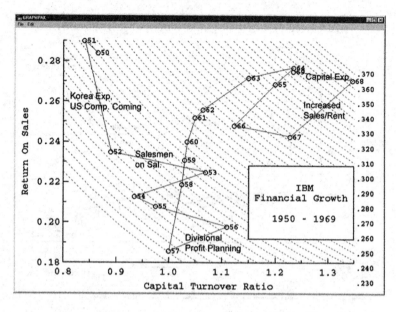

IBM Exhibit 4

1962–1966 U.S. Industrial Return on Investment
Mobley Chart

(Changed to '01-'04 for CPA Professional Education)

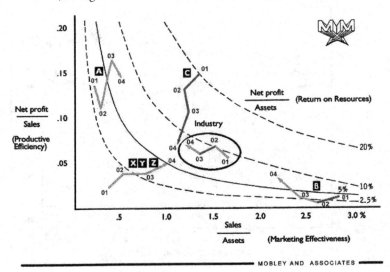

IBM Exhibit 5

ROA Graph Pencil Worksheet

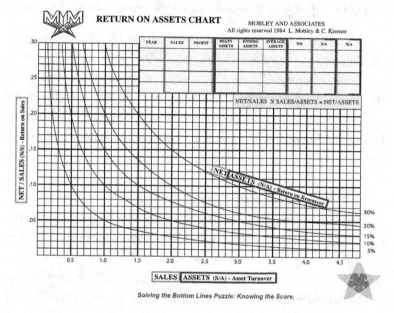

Solving the Bottom Lines Puzzle: Knowing the Score.

Access this template at www.MOSupgrade.com/MLA/Library

If ROA results do not fall within the limits of the chart above, extend the few darker lines either down proportionally to reflect losses or over to the right to reflect asset turnover of over 5 percent.

"Sacred Glossary"

A Behavioral and Financial Glossary, and Why Enterprises Need a Sacred One (find page 3 on at www.MOSupgrade.com/MLA/Library)

Consider a few paragraphs from Chuck Kremer in *Managing by the Numbers*. His insights are followed by an alphabetical list of key terms used in *Mastering Leadership Alignment,* with which readers may not be familiar. We encourage collaborative examination of all the elements that make up a shared language. For value creation in the enterprise work system to flourish, decide what words and meaning go in the enterprise "dictionary," and then use it to evolve further collaboration.

From Chuck Kremer, CPA . . .

"Accountants and financial people like myself are notorious for using different terminology for the same concepts or items on a financial statement. Should the top line on an income statement be labeled 'sales' or 'revenues'? Is the income statement itself called that—or is it the 'profit-and-loss statement' or 'statement of operations'? Is the bottom line on that statement (whatever you name it) called 'profit after tax' or 'net profit' or 'net earnings' or 'net income'?

And if you really want to start a debate, just ask a roomful of accountants to define the term 'free cash flow'. You could come back in a few days and the arguments wouldn't be over.

We cannot change this fact. But we do urge you to adopt one set of terms for your own company and never deviate from it. Pick a word for the bottom line on an income statement—we happen to like 'net profit,' but you can choose whatever you like—and *stick* to it. Always use that term to refer to that line item. Do the same thing with all the other line items on the financial statements. If your balance sheet contains the entry 'net property, plant, and equipment'—and if you like that term—then remember that this is the same as 'net fixed assets' but do not *call* the item net fixed assets. Call it net property, plant, and equipment. Always!

Why? Financial statements and financial terminology are complicated enough. People get confused when there's no need. Just pick one set of terms and stick to it. When you communicate with your accountant, your managers, and your employees, use your *sacred financial glossary* and never deviate from it. It will make communication much clearer and hence much easier."

All the Elements

Chuck's insights about the need for an explicit dictionary of commonly used financial terms also extend to the behavioral and cultural terms. Underlying all other attempts at alignment, if you want it to sustain and grow in unanimity, build a dictionary together of the core terms you use to create value as an enterprise.

Here are definitions of terms used in *Mastering Leadership Alignment*

Ballard's Alignment and Reporting Disciplines Glossary

(CC) Ballard/Commons/PMI. 2012 and 2014 or Trademarked/Registered

Sacred Glossary: A core concept distinguished and developed by Chuck Kremer, CPA, to describe the basic financial mindset and key vocabulary for value creation in an enterprise, which is usually not defined in any formal way. He urged senior leaders to formally adopt one set of terms for its measurement accounts, summary statements and concepts, both financial and operational. His thesis is that by agreeing on a "sacred glossary" of key terms, a crucial and foundational language for success is established that will support the entire enterprise's effectiveness. (See the page at the end of this document, and/or Appendix 3, page 179 of *Managing by the Numbers,* Inc./Perseus, 2000, for more of Chuck's insights.)

Accrual Accounting: In which revenues are recorded when a product or service has been provided even if the revenues are not yet collected (normally because of customer credit agreements)

Ballard Method: Practicing Ballard's Alignment and Reporting Disciplines. The method implements practices measuring Value Creation within a comprehensive value framework. That value creation framework can be linked mathematically to the financial transactions through the Chart of (Financial) Accounts, thereby presenting a complete picture of how the value people create every day becomes the total set of financial outcomes and customer results.

Banker's Pro Forma: Financial projections of a Balance Sheet and an Income Statement fully reconciled with future cash flows. It delivers a validated risk assessment, that when made by a banker, shows that a potential loan recipient can perform on loan repayment covenants.

Go to Appendices at www.MOSupgrade.com/MLA/Library for Glossary 4B-Z.

BARD Reading List—MLA Library

In 1494, a Franciscan friar by the name of Luca Pacioli, published the 2nd book ever published, after the Bible, on the Gutenberg press, becoming the western world's first published author. He assembled a math textbook called the *Summa de Arithmetica*, which in addition to fundamental material on mathematics, proportion and perspective, included a chapter called Computaris et Scriptaris (Computing and Writing). By recording what had been known for scenturies as 'The Venetian Method', he made a lasting contribution to western civilization, documenting a method of recording assets (distinguished from income or expense) by building a Balance Sheet derived through double-entry bookkeeping. What he documented then is not so different in structure from the accounting we use today. This book and those below add dimensions to numbers reporting that deliver practical transparency, so anyone in an enterprise can have access to numbers that are alive for them, not just the trained experts.

Managing by the Numbers: A Commonsense Guide to Understanding and Using Your Company's Financials, Kremer et al, Inc./Perseus, NY, 2000—Core Financial Scoreboard (FSB) Excel® Template Demonstration & "User's Manual" with SOHO Case numbers in Scoreboard form. Everyone interested in building a stronger business needs to understand and use the information captured in financial statements. In *Managing by the Numbers*, business education and accounting experts Chuck Kremer and Ron Rizzuto team up with open-book management authority John Case to demystify the numbers. They present a practical, common-sense approach to reading financial statements and to managing the three bottom lines of business financial performance: operating cash flow, net profit, and return on asset stewardship. The book features numerous exercises and examples (with associated templates available at mosupgrade .com), a powerful new management tool known as "The Financial Scoreboard," and an extensive glossary. Managing by the Numbers is an essential resource for entrepreneurs, business owners, managers, and anyone eager to improve their mastery of the financial side of running a business.

The Art of Focused Conversation (Stansfield et al, ICA Canada, Toronto, 1997)

Provides 100 ways to access group wisdom in the workplace, and is intended to expand images of what can be accomplished through the Focused Conversation Method. It demonstrates how many workplace tasks can be accomplished through the medium of focused conversation. BARD is a highly specific new form of what is offered in 25 pages of text and 100 killer agendas in the book. BARD is what it is today due in large part to Jahn Ballard learning and using this method professionally since 1987 and using it as the underlying design guide for BARD.

Transforming Performance Measurement: Rethinking the Way We Measure and Drive Organizational Success, Spitzer AMACOM, NY, 2007—Value Creation Accounting "User's Manual"
Accurately measuring performance—of individuals, departments, projects, and initiatives—is the single best way to ensure strong, sustainable results. But many organizations have flawed or inconsistent measurement systems, which can lead to waste, dissatisfaction, and loss. *Transforming Performance Measurement* helps organizations maximize the value of their performance measurement approaches by offering a "Path to Measurement Maturity," which is in perfect alignment with the CEO Reality Check and MOS Upgrade.

Deep Smarts: How to Cultivate and Transfer Enduring Business Wisdom, **Leanard & Swap,** Harvard Business School Press, Boston, 2005
Authors Leonard and Swau assert that 50 percent or more of enterprise value-creating assets exist in the minds and direct daily experience of the staff. Whether they leave for today or forever, when they do, their tacit job knowledge leaves with them. The authors cogently demonstrate that the general inabilities of businesses and institutions to document and transfer staff tacit job knowledge are one of the greatest weaknesses of enterprise in the US Market. The authors have a second title: *Critical Knowledge Transfer* about how to transfer your enterprise's most important knowledge—before it walks out the door.

Accountability: Freedom and Responsibility without Control, Lebow and Spitzer (not the same as above)—Berrett-Koehler, Berkeley, 2002
Authors Rob Lebow and Randy Spitzer show how to transform a business by replacing the control and manipulation that typically characterize workplace issues and personal accountability. The book helps readers

determine the level of accountability that exists in a company, discusses the "Seven S's of Accountability," and introduces the "member citizen" concept and the metaphor of the Wise Counsel—a coach, mentor, and leader who functions as a resource, not a controller.

The Goal: A Process of Ongoing Improvement, Goldratt, North River Press, CT, 1984

Written in a fast-paced thriller style, The Goal, a gripping novel, is transforming management thinking throughout the world. It is a book to recommend to your friends in industry—even to your bosses—but not to your competitors. Alex Rogo is a harried plant manager working ever more desperately to try to improve performance. His factory is rapidly heading for disaster. So is his marriage. He has 90 days to save his plant—or it will be closed by corporate HQ, with hundreds of job losses. It takes a chance meeting with a professor from student days—Jonah—to help him break out of conventional ways of thinking to see what needs to be done. The story of Alex's fight to save his plant is more than compulsive reading. It contains a serious message for all managers in industry and explains the ideas that underline the Theory of Constraints (TOC), developed by Elihu Goldratt.

Wheelspin: The Agile Executive's Manifesto—Accelerate Your Growth, Leverage Your Value, Beat Your Competition, Mike Richardson, No Limit Pubs, AZ, 2011

This book provides a manifesto for the Why, What, When, Where, How, and Who of agility. Using stories from his experiences as a manager, executive and CEO in the Oil and Gas, Aerospace and Automotive industries, Mike Richardson explores agility in everyday terms. He explains how aircraft accidents, the BP Oil Spill, and Toyota's safety recalls relate to enterprise leadership agility challenges. He explains the agility of a jet fighter plane and pilot to show how to use similar techniques in enterprise.

Other excellent related titles:

The Lean Management System—Joe Murli

Great Game of Business—Jack Stack

Equity: Why Employee Ownership is Good for Business—Rosen, Case and Staubus

A Stake in the Outcome—Jack Stack

Compression —Robert "Doc" Hall

A Pattern Language—Christopher Alexander
The Cobbler's Son—Jeffrey Prager
Scaling Up—Vern Harnish
Money: The Acid Test—David McConaughy
Mother Earth—Studies in Stewardship—David McConaughy

Why *Mastering Leadership Alignment's* Appendices?

The material in MLA's Appendices has been curated for the following purposes. To show a range of practical real-world details demonstrating the variety of size and function within which this MOS Upgrade (Management Operating System) and related approaches can create improbably significant value creation and Operating Cash Flow (OCF) improvements. To follow the model of MLA's most-referenced and related book, *Managing by the Numbers*, the Appendices provides opportunities for those curious about the subject to delve more deeply into related territory.

Each element offers resources on practical transparency challenges and solutions to be downloaded (see library link—www.MOSupgrade.com /MLA/Library):

Enterprise Is a 1,000-Piece Accounting Puzzle That Can Be Solved
BARD's Common-Sense Big Picture of Accounting

The 'Sacred' Glossary defines key language and meaning regarding the total system of value creation and all financial results (Activity precedes transaction in all cases).

Sample Activity Statements are 'Behaviorals' that complement and drive 'Financials' – Sample statement drafts courtesy of Osborne Coinage, Cincinnati, OH, est. 1835.

Dr. Bargerstock's letter reporting three MOS Upgrades' year one Operating Cash Flow pops averaging 79% improvement.

MLA Contributions by Thought Leader Practitioners

Chuck Kremer, CPA

Jim Huntzinger, PhD.

Dean Spitzer, PhD.

Gil Friend

Darrel Mullis

Louis B. Mobley

Rob Ptacek

Robert W. "Doc" Hall

Mike Richardson

Walt Neihof

Jeffrey Prager

Robert S. Block

MLA Contributions by Thought Leader Practitioners

Accounting for the Right Reason—Measuring Value Creation
Jim Huntzinger, author, *Lean Cost Accounting and The Roots of Lean*

Examining Productivity and Throughput
Dean Spitzer, author, *Transforming Performance Measurement* and Gil Friend, author, *The Truth About Green Business*

Cost as a Process Specification
Robert W. "Doc" Hall, author, *Compression*, co-founder, *www.compression.org*

The Use and Abuse of Financial Statement Information, 2001
Chuck Kremer, CPA, lead author, *Managing by the Numbers and Friendly Finance, Finally.*

Case Study: Financial Literacy in Global Manufacturing of Abrasives for Industrial Use
Darrel Mullis, co-author, *The Accounting Game*

PortionPac Chemical—Compression Pioneer
Robert W. "Doc" Hall, author, *Compression*, co-founder, *www.compression.org*

History of the Mobley Matrix
As told by Louis B. Mobley, lead author, *Beyond IBM*, in Friendly Finance, Finally, 1998

Cases, Articles & White Papers for further study also at:
www.MOSupgrade.com/MLA/Library

IBM Return on Investment Mapped using the DuPont Formula
Walt Neihof, *GraphPac Software, IBM (Retired)*

Leaning Away from Standard Costing—Strategic Finance, June 2016
Shi and Bargerstock, co-author, *Mastering Leadership Alignment*

Metrics-Driven Policy Deployment and Lean Sigma Continuous Improvement
Rob Ptacek, co-author, *Today's Lean Leader* and *Lean Six Sigma Pocket Guide*

How Ballard's Alignment and Reporting Disciplines Deliver Organizational Agility

Mike Richardson, author, *Wheelspin*

Seven Key Numbers: A simple framework for building profit

Jeff Prager, CEO, *Backroom Management*, author, *The Cobbler's Son*

Whole Business Thinking

Robert S., author, *Whole* Business Thinking

Friendly Finance, Finally Glossary of Terms

Chuck Kremer, lead author, *Friendly Finance*, Finally, 1998

Afterword

by Andrew Bargerstock

As I read the final manuscript of this book, I breathed a sigh of deep satisfaction. Satisfaction comes from the good fortune to have met Jahn Ballard, who has worked for so many years to fill the void of my dismay about the Missing Methodology as described in the Preface. Satisfaction brings appreciation too. I express considerable gratitude to Jahn who has become a good friend and collaborator on our path together.

I reflect back on the major influences in my life and career path as they affected my ability to contribute to this project.

My career path began fresh out of graduate school in Pittsburgh, PA, in the early 1970s when I worked as an auditor with Main, Lafrentz & Company. I deepened my understanding of what it takes to run a business effectively. I learned about *the important work of public accountants who verify the completeness and fairness of the financial statements* that we use to make investment and banking decisions.

Later, I worked for an executive search firm, Taylor Group, in Greensboro, NC, and the later in Fairfield, IA. During those few years, Ralph Taylor taught me the gifts that come from persistent commitment to goals and the attention to details. He taught me *"how to make things happen."*

In 1988, when I started my own human resource (HR) management consulting firm, Vanguard Resource Group, Inc., I learned how to bring value to corporate America as a trainer and consultant in recruitment and selection practices. With time, I saw how to bring my skills in teaching and auditing into the mix and helped develop a system to audit, measure, and improve corporate HR services. The Vanguard experiences gave me insights about *staying alert to opportunities* that come around us almost on a daily basis—opportunities that many people overlook or dismiss. Now, in my life I am fully awake to opportunity, one of which came in the form of a phone call from Jahn Ballard a few years ago.

By 1995, I completed my dissertation research leading to a PhD in Management at Maharishi University of Management in Fairfield, IA. My inspiration came from Maharishi Mahesh Yogi, whose Transcendental Meditation® (TM) technique I learned in 1972 during my MBA studies. This simple mental technique improved my mental clarity and insights while bringing deep rest to my body. Now, some 40 years later, I see that the TM practice has given me *a competitive advantage in the workplace and an easily accessible personal space of centered silence.*

In 1995, my wife and I began our second entrepreneurial venture as exclusive independent contractors for a company where within 4 years we grew our revenues to $1 million annually. Within a few years, I was asked to move into regional sales management for Books Are Fun, Ltd. (BAF), where our team of independent contractors reversed a 3-year negative growth trend and produced in the first year a 34 percent boost in revenues. In 1999, Readers Digest acquired BAF for $385 million. Within a couple of years, I found myself at the helm as the first Divisional Sales VP for Books Are Fun, who had also been an independent rep. In this scenario, our team of regional VPs and sales managers reversed a −3 percent sales trend to produce +6 percent increase in 2001, despite the severe impact of the 911 incident on sales in the prime-selling season of fall 2001. In 2002, we grew sales 15 percent year over year. From these experiences, I learned *the power of leadership, communication, and collaboration.*

Between and sometimes concurrently with these positions, I taught college and university business courses mostly in accounting and finance. Students told me that I had special talents for transforming complex topics into language and concepts that were easier to understand and apply in a practical manner.

Currently, I serve as Director of the MBA program and Chair of the Accounting Department at Maharishi University of Management (MUM) in Fairfield, IA, and Adjunct Faculty in Finance for the online MBA program at Norwich University in Northfield, VT. The years of teaching developed in me an appreciation of the enthusiasm of young people and what some have labeled as *a gift of speech and writing* that has allowed me to publish articles and speak at professional conferences in HR management and accounting topics.

In 2008, my teaching colleague at MUM, Jimmy Sinton, encouraged me to look into Lean Accounting. Jimmy was a skilled lean management consultant who I came to respect. When Jimmy spoke, I listened. This began my journey into Lean. Now, in 2016, I am a Certified Lean Management Facilitator, two-time winner of the Lean Enterprise Institute's Excellence in Lean Accounting Professor of the Year, and author of research articles published in peer-reviewed journals such as *Management Accounting Quarterly* (2011, 2013) and *Strategic Finance* (2016). But, the biggest win came in the form of two of my PhD students who were named Lean Accounting Students of the Year by the Lean Accounting Summit in 2011—Manjunath Rao in 2013 and Ye Shi (a two-time winner) in 2016. I look back with appreciation for Dr. Sandra Richtermeyer (former President of the Institute for Management Accountants) and James Huntzinger (founder of the Lean Accounting and Management Summit and President of Lean Frontiers), who both have supported our research and publications at MUM. With great gratitude to all involved in this journey, I appreciate the small measure of *acknowledgment in the fields of Lean Management and Lean Accounting* that has come my way.

All of this background may have influenced Stuart Valentine (President of Centerpoint Investment Strategies, a green investing management advisory firm with the mission of aligning wealth acquisition with social responsibility and personal development) when, after experiencing Jahn Ballard's Reality Check benefits, he recommended that Jahn contact me about collaborating on his book project.

Finally, I appreciate that Jahn Ballard took the time needed to explain his methodology for dramatically improving the connections between business planning and execution. We worked for nearly a year to get a handle on the challenge about how to best communicate the Missing Methodology to the world. Jahn's clear, systematic mind and persistence have allowed him to continue to pursue perfection of BARD. The BARD methods are intimately linked to principles of natural law that govern the evolution of open systems in nature that includes human beings and businesses, both of which exchange matter and energy with their environments. From Jahn, I learned another profound stroke that *connects natural law with business practicalities.*

To summarize, my life has been a journey of discovery and illumination that put me in a special circumstance to be able to assist Jahn Ballard in the task of communicating BARD to the world.

The organizing power of BARD fills the void of the Missing Methodology for which I have been searching since graduate school. And, now you possess this knowledge to wake up your team to a path to accomplish higher levels of business performance. Your choice now is to either lay down the book or make a commitment to implement BARD methods. I hope you will move ahead into new territory by implementing BARD! We stand ready to assist in any way.

Afterword

J.W. Ballard

Tom Hood's metaphor of the ship of value creation is apt. As the captain, he needs reliable input from leaders and crew in all parts of the ship. The ship of enterprise is laden with unopened containers of tacit knowledge and wisdom. The more self-managing the staff, the better, so they can most accurately apply the scientific method together, to conduct analysis and reporting from their view of the "ship."

Transparency Postulate: The fundamental operating deliverable for financial statements should be a clear and consistent presentation of the facts regarding property, contract, and operating performance. Statements should connect operating cash flow with both return and activity measures. Make them good tools to measure and present timely and complete facts of financial performance. The single greatest driver of unhealthy internal competition, staff conflict and leadership stress in organizational life, may be the recurring cycles of distrust and fear generated invisibly (without notice) by irrelevant, and often operationally inaccurate financial statements.

My intention for this book is to provide a primer on enterprise execution. Using the five alignment and reporting disciplines to document a common business operating language provides the capacity to build culture at work such that everyone can be involved in, and use, the enterprise value cycle; for continuous problem seeing and problem solving. The very act of people measuring impacts of their own activities at work, if sustained, inevitably translates into constructive behavior change (thanks to Doc Hall of the AME and compression.org for his very relevant input on this subject, see his insights on the book site).

There are currently (in 2016) eight extant Management Operating System (MOS) Upgrade case studies, with several more in the pipeline, which demonstrate the economic power of building unanimity on core objective facts.

The three short sections to go in this Afterword are:

- Cash Reporting and US Enterprise
- Best Practices Supporting and Complimenting BARD
- A Future of Enterprise that Works Well for Everyone

Cash Reporting and US Enterprise

US enterprises did not have a generally accepted accounting statement of bank account activity available to them from a Certified Public Accountant (CPA) until November of 1987. There had been no reporting of bank account activity in CPA licensing since the profession's inception through the SEC Acts of 1933 and 1034. The availability of cash reporting for enterprise from CPAs only exists because Lou Mobley (Tom Watson Jr.'s stand-in, internal IBM troubleshooter and executive leadership development director until retirement in 1970) crusaded for 7 years, writing letters to key influencers, to give US enterprises a direct statement of Cash Flow from Operating Activities as part of Generally Accepted Accounting Principles (GAAP).

As mentioned in Chapter 3, since 2010, studies show * that still less than 2 percent of businesses actually use the direct cash statement format Lou discovered in 1959, which details actual operating cash accounts in the bank account.

Still not available as a standard report option in QuickBooks®, the "Direct Cash Statement" format continues to be present in the GAAP, but almost entirely unused. Chuck Kremer's estimate of the cost of this deficiency is an average loss from any business over 10 to 20 people, of between 25 and 33 percent of its operating cash flow every day. His conclusions came from 20 years of doing financial literacy training with over 25,000 people in medium and large enterprises.

MOS Upgrades provided operating cash improvements averaging over a million dollars in the first year (in three cases where we had full financials for the 5-year case period). In those three enterprises of four to sixty-eight million dollars in annual revenues, the MOS upgrade delivered an average cash flow from operating activities improvement of 79 percent.

Keith Cunningham has trained thousands of small business owners who are consistently improving their financials using the Three-Bottom-Line approach. Keith proved that the Three-Bottom-Line approach enabled business people to overcome what he termed "Income Statement Addiction." He helped himself, his business owner students, and his clients achieve insanely successful financial results.

Imagine for a moment what an enterprise could do with 25 to 79 percent more cash in 1 year. It has been over 25 years since the Direct format was made "voluntary, but highly encouraged." What if US enterprises had direct activity to cash reporting to work with over the last quarter century because enterprise had its eye on the ball with cash?

- *Introduction to Financial Accounting*, 3rd Edition, by Werner and Jones, cites *Accounting Trends and Techniques* report that of the 600 enterprises it surveyed in 2001, only 7 (slightly > 1 percent) used the direct method in preparing statements of cash flows for the year 2000.

Best Practices Supporting and Complimenting BARD

Many excellent contributions made by the Lean Management disciplines have helped inform this book. Creating "standard work" that those doing the activities of that work both embrace and help evolve is also one of Lean's most value-creating methods in the mid and longer terms (while also one of the more difficult to implement). We encourage senior teams to develop standard work for building alignment and unanimity as a challenging breakthrough set of new leadership habits that will reap unimaginable rewards.

With BARD, we have invited you to imagine and to begin defining standard work for the senior team to build trust around the core facts of the enterprise. We support senior leaders to refrain from intervening with staff, when it does not forward staff's effective thought and action, but rather ask focused questions, and request new policy recommendations come in writing. Then *wait* for those written new policy proposals to come *before* giving feedback. BARD achieves this often-unattainable result (of not interfering with people's work) by structuring common sense learning and facilitation loops that people across all levels of function, authority, and experience can use as a shared documentation, alignment, and reporting skill set.

By focusing on discovering and documenting the linkages between enterprise activities and the cash flow accounts the activities directly impact, everything else in the enterprise will flow more smoothly, and feel more satisfying to each person in their role(s).

In addition to standard work definition, other current enterprise best practices that compliment and build with BARD are Policy Deployment, Balanced Scorecards with Strategy Maps, The Great Game of Business, ADKAR, Appreciative Inquiry, and Hoshin Kanri.

> *Adhocracy is a horizontal organizational structure made up of flexible hierarchies that change according to circumstances. The leadership role in a given situation is defined by skill level, experience, creativity, initiative and willingness to take responsibility.*
>
> **Alvin Toffler**

BARD will also compliment and support a host of other worthwhile methodologies, by no means limited to, but certainly including Lean Management, Deming's Quality Circles/TQM/Baldridge Award, Scanlon's Methods, Business Intelligence, Holacracy, Enterprise Resource Planning, Robert's Rules of Order, Data Warehousing, Servant Leadership, Big Data Analysis, Technology of Participation, XBRL, Six Sigma, Learning Organizations, Agile Programming and Project Management, and dozens or even hundreds more.

These and other methodologies for helping enterprises thrive can be made more effective by leveraging the tacit value creation knowledge of leaders and staff, especially in regard to linking operating activities to the transactions they impact directly.

A Future of Enterprise that Works Well for Everyone

The greatest single need of our time may be to mature the capacity of institutions (multinational corporations, businesses, governments, churches, schools, hospitals, and community benefit corporations) to serve the needs of society, the planet, and the people that work there. This will require perhaps the greatest explosion of creativity and innovation in history.

1. How can we harness the vast capacity of individuals working together to make powerful and lasting change within the crisis of collective will we are witnessing across the board in today's world, and in our workplaces?
2. What is the difference that will make the difference for more successfully generating and sustaining enterprise and economy?

Underlying any real change in collective behavior is the ability for all stakeholders to better see the objective facts of the situation, see together what is possible for the future, learn together from experience, and apply that learning effectively to overcome challenges at hand.

To you all as an entire group, my deep gratitude to all the individuals who have supported our work. There are many leaders who have contributed to Rob Lederer and myself toward offering to upgrade the Management Operating System. We are privileged to participate in learning the arts and sciences of guiding us all toward a future of enterprise and society that works well for everyone.

Productive and sustainable human endeavor hinges on building ever greater individual and group capacity to co-create environments in which everyone gives their gifts. Enterprises that can learn to allow internal trust to continuously grow are far more likely to assure that all the available wisdom is being applied to the situations at hand. Through "Enterprise Commons," where the good of the whole is always the governing context, emergent truth is an unerring guide over time. Meeting the needs of the individuals and teams, in their value-creating functions and activities, constitutes the daily reality for senior leadership to serve most directly. A far more vibrant and effective marketplace and democracy, an elusive vision so often yearned for, and so often obscured in the "current reality" of enterprise, social and political life, is within our grasp; if we will but learn together about those few key numbers that are right now already part and parcel of our daily work and service lives, even as they yet remain invisible to us.

Acknowledgments

I begin a string of acknowledgment with one whose story is known to very few. His pioneering work with leadership development over decades showed me what one highly focused and intentional individual can do to reduce and transform persistent institutional stupidity syndrome—the phenomenon of smart people in enterprise getting and staying stupid as an entire organizational entity, while also largely well intended, competent, and caring as individuals.

The Shoulders on Which I Stand:

My first acknowledgment is to my father, and one of my heroes, Jack Ballard (1927 to 2006), thought leader on the "New Impermanence," and coauthor with my mother, Phoebe, of *Beating the Age Game*, and *Turning Points*. He was also coinventor with her and my brother Michael of the *Turning Points Navigator*. Jack was the liaison from the Class of 1950 at Princeton (of which he was also past class president) to the Center for Economic Policy Studies at the University, which was a great passion for him from its inception. I had the unique opportunity and immense privilege of being witness to his leadership style and grace close-up over the period of his last 10 years as a Human Resources innovator for Mobil Corporation, from 1976 to 1986, and as Chair of the Executive Committee for a Wainwright House, personal and executive growth center. Jack was deeply committed to understanding the worlds he lived and worked in, and how to build organizational capacity to care more effectively for people. He especially focused on developing the ability to discover, direct, and manifest our own destiny as expressed by our natural genius, and care for those closest to us.

To get at the mysterious and endlessly complex question of how to positively evolve institutions, he teamed up with fellow change explorer, Norman Hirst, a brilliant artificial intelligence software entrepreneur, designer, and whole systems philosopher who had a research fellowship with IBM. They convened a brain trust called the Ishinoya Circle at Wainwright House, a Center for the Development of Human Resources, so named in 1971. Around the same time he renamed his job at Mobil International from Personnel Director to Human Resources Director. The learning circle engaged a dozen or more consultants, authors, and executives, who included Gifford Pinchot, author of *Intrapreneuring*, and Bob Schwartz of the Tarrytown Conference Center. Also participating was my mother, Pheobe Ballard, M.A., who served Wainwright as both program director and assistant director, and accompanied Jack to thought leadership events around the globe.

I have been using three documents my father was part of creating as the foundation for three decades of my own action-research experiments, the last two of which have been focused on developing BARD and the MOS Upgrade. The first and foremost is Jack's January, 1984 *Institutional Learning and Development Précis* of the second document, *Report from Task Force 1*, June, 1983, written by Norman Hirst, and edited by Jack. The third is a report from May 1984, which Jack wrote about the *Third Conference on Appropriate Governance* at Esalen Institute (scans are available upon request). All three of these documents were informed by his whole career, and influenced strongly by a large project he was engaged in at the time.

This significant 4-year project of Jack's was to transfer the capacity to manage all aspects of drilling and refining operations from the expatriate trained experts and staff in Saudi Arabia to the local employees. This massively complicated and challenging cross-cultural training and capacity-building project was perhaps one of the largest of its kind yet undertaken. To win the contract, Mobil International had competed directly with the largest consulting firms in the world. They had won based on the Human Resources management infrastructure Jack had created for the International Division's 3,000 executives in over 100 countries. His model shifted the role of direct reports away from directive, command, and control leadership, and toward more of a nondirective role as coach, capacity-builder, and mentor. In the early 1970s, this project and his previous work within Mobil represented some significant institutional progress toward addressing issues of care and respect for the human resources in an enterprise.

I stand today on the shoulders of other heroes and mentors who made long-term contributions to my work on alignment and reporting disciplines, which Andy Bargerstock has so generously supported and helped define.

Prior to thanking all those people who have directly supported this work, I want to extend an appreciation to an individual, who was also a giant among men, whom I had the privilege of knowing the rest of his life after 1994, who was very receptive and encouraging.

As I have been privileged to work with and be around personal computers since the RS 80, the SOL 20 and Apple 1, and ran our Mobley Matrix market introduction demos in 1986 on the original dual-floppy disc IBM and Kaypro machines, my appreciation for Douglas 'Doug' Engelbart knows no bounds.

Doug held a vision from 1944 on when he had visions of a personal interface with his radar screen, which has become for many of us, a major defining part of our lives. Doug and his team gave us everything we do with personal computers, from the mouse to most computer functionalities. In 1968 he demonstrated over 20 entirely new innovations defining personal computing to this day. Even now, we use less than ¾'s of those breakthroughs he demonstrated. Knowing Doug, having the benefit of his counsel, was profoundly validating for me, and a source of inspiration to continue what has turned out to 2 to 3 decades of work to get this book done right, depending on how one measures it.

He understood my practical transparency work immediately, and in a very complete way. Doug agreed that the practical transparency with measurement we are introducing was the missing piece in his 'Bootstrapping Method' (a learning and innovation method using what some of his fellow practitioners named triple-loop learning). By not having a fourth loop of transparent measurement, Bootstrapping had not enabled itself to propagate much beyond his Augmentation Research Center at Stanford Research Institute in the 1960's, with unlimited funding underwritten by both NASA and DoD, from whence he and his team delivered the 'Mother of all Demos' to thousands of engineers.

My appreciation also goes out to a colleague of Doug's, Jim Spohrer, of IBM Services Research, who first used our Financial Dashboard in his presentations to illustrate a fourth learning loop - measurement. And to my friend and colleague, Dixon de Lena, who was gracious enough to accompany me to my first visit with Jim at Almaden to share the dashboard and value creation tools.

Jim was kind enough to introduce me to Dean Spitzer, whose seminal work, *Transforming Performance Measurement*, is a master text in the *Mastering Leadership Alignment* Library. Dean's generosity of his material to this project has added no-fee value creation assessments for all of our use. I am so grateful to Dean for our collaborating in highly creative and effective ways, his direct support of my clients, and for requesting his publisher grant us rights to use with attribution, the three value creating assets assessments in his book. It is recommended our clients buy a personal copy of *Transforming Performance Measurement* for each member of their upgrade team, in addition to *Managing by the Numbers*, and this book.

Thanks to my clients who have trusted me to deliver value in a way they had never heard of before, and who have allowed me to share some of their alignment and reporting stories with others: Jeff Lueken, Randy Stark, Rick Call, Scott Leonard, and Jeff Stegman, Stuart Valentine, et al.

Tom Hood and Skip Falatco for their unfailing patience and generosity since we first met in 2001, and for being CPA leaders so committed to adding value to CPA services to the market. To Tom for his unique leadership, his passion for the ROA Graph, and crucial contribution to the Krermer/Hood Performance Measures Assessment.

Gene Bazan, who has generously shared his wisdom and methods with me since 1998, and without whose assistance, I would not have had this book in this form nor the methods this refined.

Rob Lederer, Principal at Management Resources, a founding "B" Corporation, and good friend. Rob and Jahn are creating the distinction of a Management Operating System and its upgrade. For the better part of a decade, Rob has been a wonderful consistent fellow deep thinker and actor about leadership alignment and reporting disciplines. Thank you so much Rob. And to our mutual colleague, Dixon de Lena for knowing the tow of us should meet back in 2007.

Jim Tait, General Manager and General Counsel for Performance Management Institute, has been a miraculous rock for years now. Words cannot convey my gratitude for his gracious and generous support on too many levels to name, nor for my admiration for his leadership as Chief of Staff for Governor Reuben Askew, when they helped guide the State of Florida to a bi-partisan re-writing of its state constitution in the 1970's.

Andy Gin, a physician and neurologist from Oklahoma City, who found me through John Case, a coauthor with Chuck Kremer and Ron Rizzuto of *Managing by the Numbers*. He wanted to use the Financial Scoreboard and the book in his role as an adjunct business school professor of healthcare enterprise management in an Executive MBA Program at the University of Oklahoma City. Through weekly conversations since 2007, Andy has been a most valued advisor, friend, and a connector. His continued board service shows his commitment to helping leaders to effectively use the resources they already have.

Working on this book with Andy Bargerstock has been one of the most productive and creative collaborations. It has ever been my privilege to be part of it. I am eternally grateful for his enthusiasm for our subject, as well as his generosity and wisdom.

I also stand on the shoulders of several heroes and mentors who have made seminal contributions to the practice of organizational learning and change, and are no longer with us.

Louis R. Mobley (1917 to 1987), founding staff and director of IBM's Sands Point Executive School from 1955 to 1970. Lou was the discoverer of the Mobley Matrix, author of *Beyond IBM*, and contributor of the Direct Format Cash Statement as codified in Financial Accounting Standards Board Regulation 95. Lou was a great friend and mentor. I was never tired of collaborating with him to bring cash-flow common sense to US enterprise, nor to sit at the feet of such a pioneer and innovator in executive development and universal human values games.

Chuck Kremer (1945 to 2005), author of *Managing by the Numbers*, and *The Use and Abuse of the Financial Statements* white paper, and developer of the Financial Scoreboard. Lou, with whom I worked in the mid-1980s, introduced me to Chuck in 1984. Chuck and I worked closely about 15 years until his passing. Collaborating with him to perfect his Financial Scoreboard (FSB) template was deeply engaging and satisfying from the moment in 1994 when I asked him to create the FSB so we could offer it to the market. *Managing by the Numbers*, Chuck's focused vision, is this book's companion volume. It is a very well-written primer on useful finance. In less than 150 pages, a story of enterprise unfolds in numbers that hold great insight in them, insight that all-to-often goes begging in workplaces.

I am compelled to also mention my folk's mentor, great teacher, peer, and colleague of Lou Mobley, Robert K. Greenleaf, author of the seminal *Leader as Servant* and *Institution as Servant*. Greenleaf's insights on Servant Leadership have contributed so much already to ethics and integrity of our institutions over the last 5 decades. His overseeing of the Rosie the Riveter programs for FDR, and building the culture at Bell Labs in the 1950s, were both significant contributions to US enterprise. Bob and his wife Esther created the Receptive Listening course (derived from Carl Rogers), in which my parents, in 1957, received not only a method to guide their own lives and their family, but also the foundation of their work with guiding people to gracefully navigate their turning points and the "third half" of their lives.

My gratitude to my brothers, Bob Ballard, for his counsel that is always wise, and astonishing writing skills; and Mike Ballard, for his insight, humor, and support for scaling practical transparency in the market.

And to my mother, Phoebe Ballard, coauthor of *Turning Points* and *Beating the Age Game*, for her willingness to review this book as a lay person. And also both to her and her husband Dick Ford, for being 100 percent supportive of my success in bringing the MOS Upgrade to the market.

To Ruth Harris and John Locket for patiently supporting this journey for a very long time. Without Ruth's graphics and web support, who knows where this work would be.

To Robert Girling of Sonoma State University School of Business and Economics, for being a most valued colleague at the Sustainable Enterprise Conference at SoMo Village each year, and for introducing me to your publisher, and now ours as well, Scott Isenberg at Business Expert Press. Thank you Scott for your gracious hand-holding through the process of this book.

To Dave Emery for his generous and thoughtful support with the manuscript through both editing and authoring the white paper abstracts to introduce contributors to the additional resources folder offered with the book.

To Jim Huntzinger and Doc Hall for their unflagging encouragement, connections, and careers dedicated to bringing more effectiveness, satisfaction, and respect to all workplaces. To Joe Murli and Mark Hamel for strongly reinforcing the book's focus on leadership alignment.

There are two more significant and very wise presences in my life, and certainly some the most prolific, effective, and productive people I know, without whose friendship and guidance over decades the MOS Upgrade would not be where it is today.

Robert S. Block, author of *Whole Business Thinking, A Guide to Financial Management* and the *Whole Business Thinking Glossary*, whose career as an entrepreneur and inventor has spanned over a half century, with successes in many diverse fields, including and not limited to Advertising, Television, Airlines and Travel, Entertainment, Telecommunications (he patented the technology for pay-per-view and founded SelecTV), Venture Capital, and most recently, Enterprise Software. Bob was Lou Mobley's business partner in bringing the original Mobley Matrix software to market. He has invested a huge amount of his attention and resources in making enterprise tools powerfully address the challenges of organization in newly integrative ways. It has been a huge gift for me to have been able to collaborate with Bob on developing several core MOS Upgrade document templates.

My former boss and friend, Phil Arregiun of Boardroom Consultants, whose example, contributions to mitigating underfunded legacy costs, and profound insight continue as a beacon of effectiveness, globally empowering leaders across today's turbulent marketplace. Phil has always helped me keep my focus on what is really important.

To the men of the Mankind Project (mankindproject.org), my gratitude for the support I have received cannot be over-stated. I am proud to be one of over 50,000 men in dozens of countries who are pro-actively taking as full responsibility for ourselves within our spheres of influence as we possibly can. Last, but not least, there is a global social enterprise that has lived and operated with as high integrity and consistency as any of the thousands I have witnessed in four decades. Today this over 70-year-old beneficial global presence is revered by collaborative leaders the world over. Its pioneering work as, effectively, a global private peace corps with full integrity, operating for much of the last over half century on a need-to-know basis, stands as one the greatest "stories never told." The power and magnificence of inspired service to all of humankind that this thoughtful, effective, and committed group brings is awesome.

The Institute of Cultural Affairs' (www.ica-usa.org) Technology of Participation has been the most profoundly useful and joyful set of collaborative learning tools I have ever known. With the patient guidance of my friend, colleague, and mentor, Don Cramer, with great support from Marilyn Oyler, I learned to practice fun methods for evoking and applying all the available wisdom in a room or enterprise. I have come to know, love, and revere this community of social entrepreneurs whose Human Development Initiatives have touched many millions, and whose curiosity, love, and genius did much to create an emergent vocation in the last 50+ years, that of the professional facilitator.

Index

OTHER TITLES IN OUR SUPPLY AND OPERATIONS MANAGEMENT COLLECTION

Joy M. Field, Boston College, *Editor*

- *Understanding the Complexity of Emergency Supply Chains* by Matt Shatzkin
- *Contemporary Issues in Supply Chain Management and Logistics* by Anthony M. Pagano and Mellissa Gyimah
- *The Unified Theory of Profitability: 25 Ways to Accelerate Growth Through Operational Excellence* by Andrew Miller
- *Demand Forecasting for Managers* by Stephan Kolassa and Enno Siemsen
- *Managing Commodity Price Risk: A Supply Chain Perspective, Second Edition* by George A. Zsidisin, Janet L. Hartley, Barbara Gaudenzi, and Lutz Kaufmann
- *Forecasting Fundamentals* by Nada Sanders
- *1+1 = 100: Achieving Breakthrough Results Through Partnerships* by Rick Pay

Announcing the Business Expert Press Digital Library

Concise e-books business students need for classroom and research

This book can also be purchased in an e-book collection by your library as

- a one-time purchase,
- that is owned forever,
- allows for simultaneous readers,
- has no restrictions on printing, and
- can be downloaded as PDFs from within the library community.

Our digital library collections are a great solution to beat the rising cost of textbooks. E-books can be loaded into their course management systems or onto students' e-book readers. The **Business Expert Press** digital libraries are very affordable, with no obligation to buy in future years. For more information, please visit **www.businessexpertpress.com/librarians**. To set up a trial in the United States, please email **sales@businessexpertpress.com**.